PRIMARY SPONSORS TO THE EXHIBITION

National Endowment for the Humanities

Asian Art Museum of San Francisco

The Korean Traders Scholarship Foundation

Asian Art Foundation of San Francisco

The Chevron Companies

The San Francisco Foundation

City and County of San Francisco, Hotel Tax Fund

The Museum Society

The Society for Asian Art

Union Oil Company of California Foundation

Bankamerica Foundation

5,000 Years of Korean Art

한국미술오천년

An exhibition organized by the National Museum of Korea
for the following museums in the United States:

Asian Art Museum of San Francisco, May 1–September 30, 1979

Seattle Art Museum, November 1, 1979–January 13, 1980

The Art Institute of Chicago, February 16–April 27, 1980

Cleveland Museum of Art, June 10–August 10, 1980

Museum of Fine Arts, Boston, September 16–November 30, 1980

The Metropolitan Museum of Art, New York, January 5–March 15, 1981

William Rockhill Nelson Gallery of Art—Atkins Museum of Fine Arts,
Kansas City, April 17–June 14, 1981

KOREAN COMMITTEE OF HONOR
for the Exhibition "5,000 Years of Korean Art"

Mademoiselle Park Keun Hae
Chong Wa Dae

The Honorable Choi Kyu Hah
Prime Minister

The Honorable Kim Seong Jin
Minister of Culture and Information

The Honorable Kim Yong Shik
Ambassador to the United States

Dr. Lee Sun Keun
President
The Academy of Korean Studies

The Honorable Park Choong Hoon
Chairman
The Korean Traders Scholarship Foundation

UNITED STATES COMMITTEE OF HONOR
for the Exhibition "5,000 Years of Korean Art"

The Vice-President
and
Mrs. Walter F. Mondale

The Honorable Cyrus Vance
Secretary of State

The Honorable William H. Gleysteen, Jr.
Ambassador to the Republic of Korea

The Honorable Richard L. Sneider
Former Ambassador
to the Republic of Korea

The Honorable Joseph D. Duffey
Chairman
National Endowment for the Humanities

KOREAN PLANNING COMMITTEE

Dr. Kim Doo Jong, Chairman of the First Subcommittee of the Cultural Properties Committee of the Republic of Korea

Dr. Kim Chewon, Member of the National Academy of Sciences, the Republic of Korea

Mr. Choi Sunu, Director of the National Museum of Korea, Member of the Cultural Properteis Committee of the Republic of Korea

Dr. Kim Won-yong, Professor of Seoul National University, Member of the Cultural Properties Committee of the Republic of Korea

Dr. Hwang Su-young, Dean, Graduate School, Dongguk University, Member of the Cultural Properties Committee of the Republic of Korea

Dr. Chin Hongsup, Professor of Ewha Woman's University

Mr. Lee Ki-baek, Professor of Sogang University

Dr. Youn Moo-byong, Professor of Chungnam University

SAN FRANCISCO PLANNING COMMITTEE

William P. Scott, Jr., Chairman
Alexander D. Calhoun, Jr., Vice-Chairman
Choi Kyu-jang, Cultural Attaché, Consulate General, Republic of Korea
René-Yvon Lefebvre d'Argencé, Director and Chief Curator, Asian Art Museum of San Francisco
Mrs. George T. Brady, Jr.
Lorrie Bunker, Public Relations Director, Asian Art Museum of San Francisco
John B. Dowty, Assistant Director-Administrative, Asian Art Museum of San Francisco
Dr. Seymour Farber
George Hopper Fitch
James M. Gerstley, Chief Financial Officer
William E. Goetze
Jerome W. Hull, Chairman, Logistics Committee
Mrs. Albert E. Kern, Jr.
Mrs. Philip J. McCoy, Chairperson, Korean Symposium Committee
Donald R. Meyer
Mrs. Robert Seller, Chairperson, Special Events Committee
Clarence F. Shangraw, Senior Curator, Asian Art Museum of San Francisco
Mrs. Walter Shorenstein, Chairperson, Opening Night Committee
Diana Turner, Curator of Education, Asian Art Museum of San Francisco
Mrs. Brayton Wilbur, Jr.
K. L. Woo

U.S.-KOREA WORKING COMMITTEE FOR "5,000 YEARS OF KOREAN ART"

René-Yvon Lefebvre d'Argencé, Director and Chief Curator, Asian Art Museum of San Francisco, Chairman

Lorrie Bunker, Public Relations Director, Asian Art Museum of San Francisco

Choi Kyu-jang, Cultural Attaché, Consulate General, Republic of Korea

Choi Sunu, Director, The National Museum of Korea, Seoul

Ralph T. Coe, Director, William Rockhill Nelson Gallery of Art—Atkins Museum of Fine Arts, Kansas City

Ellen P. Conant, Korea Council, The Asia Society Inc., New York

John B. Dowty, Assistant Director-Administrative, Asian Art Museum of San Francisco

Wen Fong, Special Consultant for Far Eastern Affairs, The Metropolitan Museum of Art, New York

Jan Fontein, Director and Curator of Asiatic Art, Museum of Fine Arts, Boston

Jack E. Foss, Registrar, Asian Art Museum of San Francisco

Sherman E. Lee, Director and Chief Curator of Oriental Art, Cleveland Museum of Art

Lee Soo Jung, Director of Planning Department, Korean Overseas Information Service, Ministry of Culture and Information, Republic of Korea

Jack V. Sewell, Curator of Oriental Art, The Art Institute of Chicago

Clarence F. Shangraw, Senior Curator, Asian Art Museum of San Francisco

Milton R. Stern, Dean, University of California Berkeley Extension

Henry Trubner, Associate Director, Seattle Art Museum

Diana Turner, Curator of Education, Asian Art Museum of San Francisco

6

TABLE OF CONTENTS

MESSAGES

From the Minister of Culture and Information of the Republic of Korea:

"한국 미술 오천년전"이 1979년 5월부터 이태동안 미국에서 열리게 된 것을 매우 기쁘게 생각 합니다.

우리는 과학문명의 놀라운 발달로 나라와 나라사이의 물리적거리가 나날이 줄어들고 있는 시대에 살고 있읍니다. 나라사이의 거리에 못지않게 국민과 국민간의 마음의 거리도 좁혀져야 함은 두말할 나위도 없읍니다. 그길은 서로의 역사와 문화를 이해하고 사랑하는데서 찾아야 한다고 믿읍니다. 따지고 보면 어느민족의 문화와 역사이건 그것은 우리 인류가 다같이 간직하고 향유 해야할 인류공동의 자산이기 때문 입니다.

이번 전시회를 통해 우리의 미국 친구들이 우리의 염원과 재능과 가치관을 이해 하는데 도움이 된다면 그보다 다행한 일은 없겠읍니다. 본인은 이번 전시회와 같은 문화적 접촉과 교류가 더욱 활발하여 두나라 국민간의 이해와 친선이 증진 되기를 희망하는 바입니다.

이번 전시회가 실현될수 있도록 성원을 아끼지 않은 미국정부와 미연방 문화예술원 그리고 풍부한 상상력으로 갖가지 어려움을 극복하여 성공적인 전시회로 이끈 일곱개 미국측 참가 박물관 여러분에게 이자리를 빌어 감사의 뜻을 표합니다.

대한민국 문화공보부 장관

김 성 진
김 성 진

It is my great pleasure to have the exhibition "5,000 Years of Korean Art" on tour in the United States for two years beginning in May of 1979. The spatial distances between nations is fast shrinking owing to incredible developments in science and technology. Yet distances in understanding between peoples must still be narrowed. Understanding other peoples must come from an understanding of their history and culture. In the final assessment, the history and culture of any people must be considered the common wealth of all mankind.

I feel that this exhibition affords a most fortunate opportunity to permit our American friends to come close to the hopes, values and artistic talents of the Korean people. It is my wish that increased cultural contacts of this nature will follow and serve to deepen understanding and strengthen the friendship between our peoples.

I wish to take this opportunity to extend my deepest gratitude to the Government of the United States, the National Endowment for the Humanities, for their generous support of the exhibition, and to the seven great museums which, with imagination and ingenuity, have overcome numerous difficulties to make it a success.

Seoul, Korea, January 15, 1979   Kim Seong Jin

From the Secretary of State of the United States of America:

I am pleased to welcome to the United States this extensive exhibition of Korean art, a collection which reveals the depth and range of Koreans' artistic achievements over the centuries. The distinguished pieces we see here are the expression of an artistic flair which is very much alive in Korea today. I am confident that it will serve to awaken in those who view it an appreciation of a major Asian artistic tradition of which we have long known too little.

I congratulate the Government of the Republic of Korea for successfully bringing together such an ambitious undertaking and I know that my fellow citizens will take full advantage of this opportunity for a revealing look at a rich cultural tradition.

Washington, January 15, 1979

Cyrus Vance

본인은 여러세기에 걸쳐 한국 국민이 이룩한 한국 미술의 진면모를 드러낼 대규모의 한국 미술 전시회가 미국에서 열리게 된것을 충심으로 환영합니다. 우리가 이곳에서 보게 되는 찬란한 문화재는 오늘날 한국에서 생생히 엿볼수 있는 한국인들의 예술적 재능의 표현입니다. 본인은 이번 전시회를 관람하는 여러분들이 우리가 오래동안 별로 알지 못했던 중요한 동양미술의 전통을 감상할수 있는 계기가 될것을 확신합니다.

본인은 이같은 원대한 사업을 미국에서 성공적으로 추진한 대한민국 정부에 축하를 보내며 아울러 친애하는 미국 국민들이 이번 기회를 충분히 이용하여 풍부한 문화전통을 소상히 볼수있게 될것을 의심치 않습니다.

미합중국 국무 장관   사이러스. 밴스

ACKNOWLEDGMENTS

The scope and nature of the exhibition "5,000 Years of Korean Art" are such that the present volume required the unselfish participation of an unusually large number of Korean, American and Canadian scholars.

Some of these scholars have submitted drafts covering whole sections of the exhibition, others have contributed to the introduction, others again have served as mapmakers, bibliographers, consultants or reviewers. The editors feel enormously indebted to all these scholars and only regret that their valuable essays and comments could not be published in their entirety or original form.

In order to satisfy rather stringent space requirements and to provide the reader with the structural balance and stylistic homogeneity which are expected from exhibition catalogues, some considerable rewriting had to be done by the editors. They alone assume full responsibility for the inexactitudes, lacunae or defects that the final text may present.

General Editor: René-Yvon Lefebvre d'Argencé, Asian Art Museum of San Francisco.

Editor: Diana Turner, Asian Art Museum of San Francisco.

CONTRIBUTORS:
Introduction: d'Argencé; Kim Won-yong, Seoul National University; Lena Kim Lee, Hong-Ik University; Richard Pearson, University of British Columbia.
Neolithic-Bronze-Iron Ages: d'Argencé, Nos. 1-11; Pearson, Nos. 1-11; Youn Moo-byong, Ch'ungnam National University, Nos. 1-11.
Three Kingdoms: d'Argencé, Nos. 12-80; Terese Tse Bartholomew, Asian Art Museum of San Francisco, Nos. 65-66; Chin Hong-sup, Ewha Woman's University, Nos. 39-49, 50, 51, 53, 54, 63, 64; Hwang Su-young, Dongguk University, Nos. 69-80; Kim, Nos. 12-38, 52, 55-61; Kim Lee, Nos. 68-80; Stephen Little, Asian Art Museum of San Francisco, Nos. 69-80; Pearson, Nos. 12-68; Clarence F. Shangraw, Asian Art Museum of San Francisco, Nos. 67-68; Youn, Nos. 62, 65-68.
Unified Silla: d'Argencé, Nos. 81-103, Bartholomew, Nos. 98-100; Chin, Nos. 81, 95-96, 102-103; Hwang, Nos. 82-89, 92; John C. Jamieson, Stanford-Berkeley Joint East Asia Center, University of California, Berkeley, No. 96; Kim, Nos. 90-91; Kim Lee, Nos. 81-96; Little, Nos. 81-92; Pearson, Nos. 81-103; Shangraw, Nos. 96-103; Youn, Nos. 97-101.
Koryŏ: Ahn Hwi-Joon, Hong-Ik University, No. 158; d'Argencé, No. 154; Bartholomew, Nos. 127-128; Chin, Nos. 107-109, 155-156; Choi Sunu, National Museum of Korea, Nos. 111-154; Hwang, Nos. 104, 105a-b, 157; Kim Lee, Nos. 104-110, 155-162; Shangraw, Nos. 128, 139-140, 145, 151-153; Turner, Nos. 104-162.
Yi: Ahn, Nos. 181-197, 219-239, 243-245; Chung Yang-mo, National Museum of Korea, Nos. 163-180, 198-218; Holly Holtz, Asian Art Museum of San Francisco, Nos. 181-197, 219-256; Sungmii Lee Han, Doctoral Candidate, Princeton University, entries in painting section (Nos. 181-197, 219-256); Kim Lee, entries in painting section (Nos. 181-197, 219-256); Peter H. Lee, University of Hawaii at Manoa, inscriptions on some paintings in painting section (Nos. 181-197, 219-256); Turner, Nos. 163-180, 198-218.

REVIEWERS: Kenneth K. S. Ch'en, Emeritus, University of California, Los Angeles, Nos. 69-92, 104-110, 155-160; Holtz, entire manuscript; Jamieson, Introduction, Nos. 1, 3, 62-68, 97-103, 163-180, 198-218; Yoshiko Kakudo, Asian Art Museum of San Francisco, all Japanese references; Kumja Kim, Doctoral Candidate, Stanford University, entire manuscript; Kim Lee, entire manuscript; Little, entire manuscript; Michael Rogers, University of California, Berkeley, Introduction; Shangraw, Nos. 104-154, 163-174.

PHOTOGRAPHS:
Color Transparencies: Cover and I, II, V-VII, IX-XI, XV, XVI, XVIII, XX, XXIII, XXX, XXXI, XXXIII-XXXV, XXXVII-XL. Courtesy of the National Museum of Korea.
Color Transparencies: III, IV, VIII, XII-XIV, XVII, XIX, XXI, XXII, XXIV-XXVIII, XXIX, XXXII, XXXVI. Courtesy James Medley, Asian Art Museum of San Francisco.
Black and White Negatives: Frontispiece (45) and 1, 2, 4, 5, 7, 9-15, 17, 19, 22, 24, 26, 28-30, 32a, 33, 37-41, 43, 44, 46-54, 58-73, 75, 76, 80, 84, 86-90, 93, 94, 98-101, 103-105, 108, 110, 113-115, 119, 121, 129-135, 137-141, 145, 148, 150-155, 160, 163, 164, 167-172, 174, 177, 179, 181b-d, 184-193, 196, 197, 199-202, 204-207, 209-211, 213-215, 217, 218, 220-222, 226, 228-230, 233, 234, 237, 238a, 239-245, 248. Courtesy of the National Museum of Korea.
Black and White Negatives: 3, 16, 18, 21, 25, 27, 31, 32b-d, 42, 74, 78, 82, 83, 92, 95, 97, 106, 107, 112, 120, 127, 128, 142-144, 146, 147, 159, 161, 162, 175, 176, 178, 180, 181a, 182, 183, 191, 195, 198, 212, 216, 223-225, 227, 231, 232, 235, 236, 238b and detail, 246, 247, 254. Courtesy James Medley.
Printing of Negatives: Sharon Deveaux, Asian Art Museum of San Francisco.

LAYOUT AND DESIGN: d'Argencé; Turner.

COVER CALLIGRAPHY: Kim Choong Hyun.

Maps: Bartholomew; Little; Rogers.
Chronology Chart: d'Argencé; Shangraw.
Transcription of Korean Words, Names, Places: Lee; Rogers.
Selected Bibliography: d'Argencé; Chung; Jamieson; Kim Lee; Pearson.
Manuscript: Irene Handlin and Walter Schweiger, Asian Art Museum of San Francisco.

We would like to express our gratitude to all our colleagues at the National Museum of Korea.

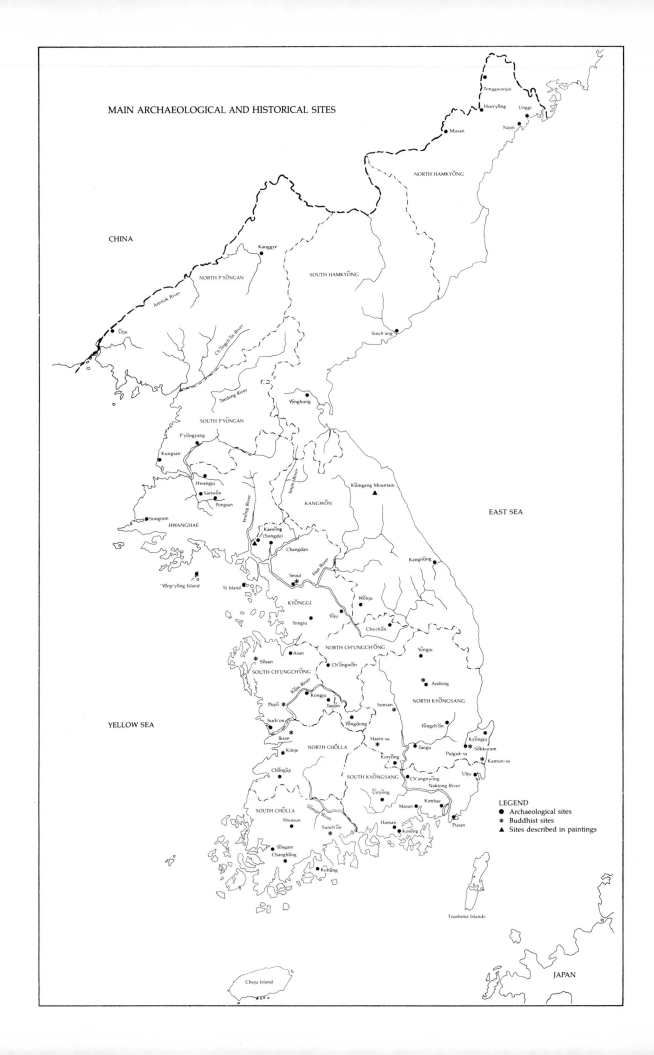

MAIN ARCHAEOLOGICAL AND HISTORICAL SITES

CHINA

Tonggwanjin
Hoeryŏng   Unggi
Musan   Najin

NORTH HAMKYŎNG

Kanggye

NORTH P'YŎNGAN   SOUTH HAMKYŎNG

Amnok River

Ch'ŏngch'ŏn River

Ŭiju   Sinch'ang

Taedong River   Yŏnghung

SOUTH P'YŎNGAN

P'yŏngyang   Kŭmgang Mountain ▲

Kungsan   Imjin River   KANGWŎN

Hwangju   Yesŏng River
Sariwŏn
Pongsan   EAST SEA

Songnim   HWANGHAE   Kaesŏng ▲
                              (Songdo)
                              Changdan   Kangnŭng
                        Seoul *   Han River
'Yŏnp'yŏng Island   Si Island
                              KYŎNGGI   Wŏnju
                        Yongiu   Yŏju
                                        Chech'ŏn
                              NORTH CH'UNGCH'ŎNG
                        Asan   Yŏngju
                    * Sŏsan
SOUTH CH'UNGCH'ŎNG   Ch'ŏngwŏn
                    Kŭm River   * Andong
                Kongju
        Puyŏ *   Taejŏn   Sonsan   NORTH KYŎNGSANG
        Soch'ŏn   Yŏngdong   *   Yŏngch'ŏn
YELLOW SEA   * Iksan   Kyŏngju
                    Kimje NORTH CHŎLLA   Haein-sa   Taegu   Pulguk-sa * Sŏkkuram
                                        Koryŏng *   Kamun-sa
            Chŏngŭp   Ulju
                        SOUTH KYŎNGSANG   Ch'angnyŏng
                              Naktong River
                                    Ŭiryŏng   LEGEND
                    SOUTH CHŎLLA   Sŏmjin River   Masan Kimhae   ● Archaeological sites
                        Hwasun   Haman   Pusan   * Buddhist sites
                              Sunch'ŏn *   Kosŏng   ▲ Sites described in paintings
                    Yŏngam
                    Changhŭng
                        Kohŭng

                                                            JAPAN

                        Tsushima Islands

Cheju Island

12

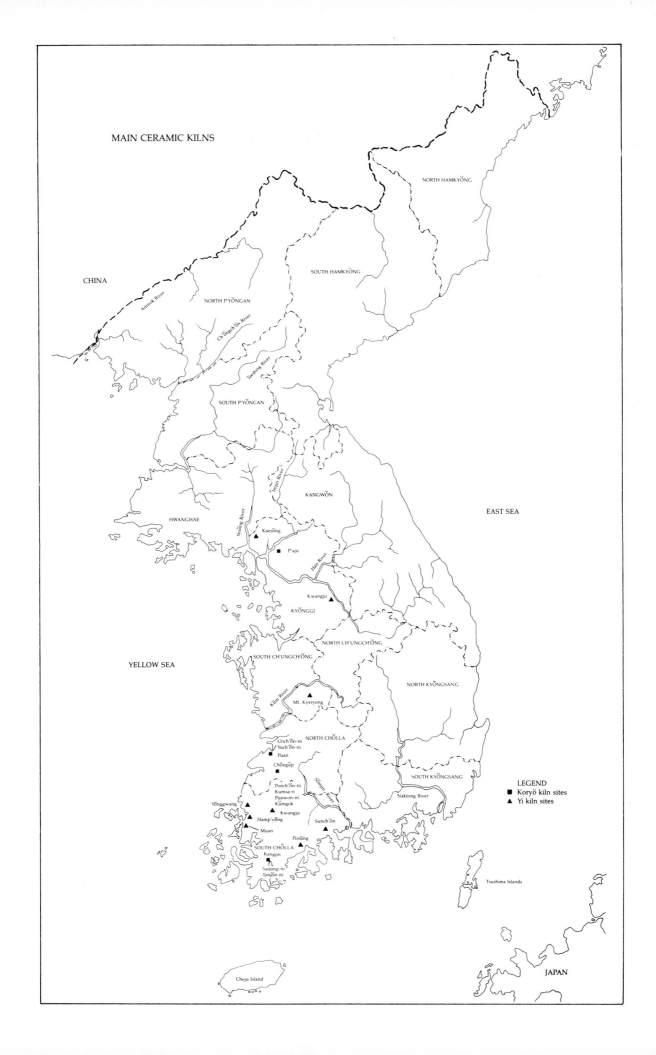

MAIN CERAMIC KILNS

CHINA

NORTH HAMKYŎNG

Amnok River

NORTH P'YŎNGAN

SOUTH HAMKYŎNG

Ch'ŏngch'ŏn River

Taedong River

SOUTH P'YŎNGAN

KANGWŎN

Imjin River

EAST SEA

Yesŏng River

HWANGHAE

▲ Kaesŏng
■ P'aju

Han River

Kwangju ▲

KYŎNGGI

NORTH CH'UNGCH'ŎNG

SOUTH CH'UNGCH'ŎNG

YELLOW SEA

NORTH KYŎNGSANG

Kŭm River

▲ Mt. Kyeryong

NORTH CHŎLLA

Unch'ŏn-ni
Yuch'ŏn-ni
■ Puan
Chŏngŭp
■

Sŏmjin River

SOUTH KYŎNGSANG

Naktong River

Punch'ŏn-ni
Kumsa-ri
Punwon-ni
Kŭmgok
Kwangju
Yŏnggwang ▲ ▲
▲ Hamp'yŏng
▲ Muan

Sunch'ŏn ▲

Posŭng ▲

SOUTH CHŎLLA
Kangjin
■
Sadang-ni
Tanjŏn-ni

LEGEND
■ Koryŏ kiln sites
▲ Yi kiln sites

Tsushima Islands

JAPAN

Cheju Island

13

COMPARATIVE CHRONOLOGY

	KOREA	CHINA	JAPAN	THE WEST
5000	*NEOLITHIC AGE*	*NEOLITHIC AGE*	*NEOLITHIC AGE* Jōmon	*NEOLITHIC AGE* Early Mesopotamia
	Comb pattern pottery	*Yang-shao and Lung-shan Cultures*		
3000		*BRONZE AGE* Shang (ca. 1523–) Chou (ca. 1027–) Western Chou (ca. 1027)		EGYPTIAN OLD KINGDOM *(Bronze Age)* *Megaliths* EGYPTIAN NEW KINGDOM (Tutankhamen) *Iron Age*
1000	*Plain coarse pottery Megaliths*	Ch'un-ch'iu (770–)		GREEK CIVILIZATION
500	*BRONZE AGE*	*Confucius (551–479?)*		Alexander the Great (356–323)
300	*IRON AGE* (Chosŏn?) *Kimhae culture* Lo-lang colony (108–)	IRON AGE Warring States (475–) CH'IN (221–) HAN (206–) *Civil Service based on Confucian training (124)*	BRONZE AGE YAYOI PERIOD	EARLY ROMAN ART
100	THREE KINGDOMS (1st century, B.C.) Old Silla (57–) Koguryŏ (37–) Paekche (18–)			
0		*Introduction of Buddhism*		
100	*Beginning of Silla pottery*			Julius Ceasar (101–44) *Destruction of Pompei (79) Construction of Pantheon (118)*
200		THREE KINGDOMS (221–) SIX DYNASTIES (265–)		*Baths of Caracalla (215)*
300	*Fall of Lo-lang (313) Tongsu tomb, Anak-kun, Hwanghae Province (357) Beginning of Buddhism in Koguryŏ (372) Beginning of Buddhism in Paekche (384)*	*Beginning of Buddhist Art* *Ku K'ai-chih (ca. 344–406) Tun-huang caves Yün-kang caves*	IRON AGE OLD TOMBS PERIOD *Haniwa Sueki* First Paekche envoy (367) Japanese invasion of Paekche and Silla (391)	*Arch of Constantine (305)*
400	*Royal Tumuli in Silla (through 6th century)*	*Lung-men caves*		Fall of Roman Empire (476)
500	*Beginning of Buddhism in Silla (528) Foundation of Pulguk-sa (532)* Death of King Munyŏng (523) Fall of Kaya (562)		*Introduction of Buddhism from Paekche (538)* ASUKA (552–) *Hōryūji* NARA (645–)	Mohammed (570–632); Hejira (622) and beginning of Islamic era
600	Fall of Paekche (660) Fall of Koguryŏ (668) UNIFIED SILLA (668–) *Construction of Anap-chi Pond (679) Foundation of Confucian University (682) Foundation of Kamŭn-sa (682) Introduction of Hwaŏm Sect of Buddhism*	SUI (589–) T'ANG (618–)		EARLY BYZANTINE ART
700	*Construction of Sŏkkuram (751)*	*First porcelains made*	*Introduction of Kegon Sect of Buddhism (735) Tōdaiji* HEIAN (794–)	Poitiers (732) Foundation of Bagdad (762) Charlemagne (768–814) EARLY MEDIEVAL ART
800				

	KOREA	CHINA	JAPAN	THE WEST
900	KORYŎ (918–)	FIVE DYNASTIES (906–) LIAO (907–) SUNG (960–)		
1000	Khitan raids (993–1018) *Protoceladons* *First celadons (ca. 1050)*		*Byōdōin*	ROMANESQUE ART First Crusade (1096)
1100	Sung Envoy Hsü Ching's visit (1123) *Inlaid Celadons (ca. 1150)*	*Neo-Confucianism* *Ma Yüan* *Hsia Kuei* *Liang K'ai*	*Tale of Gen* KAMAKURA (1185–)	GOTHIC ART *Chartres (1194)*
1200	Mongol (Yüan) invasions (1231–1239) *First use of movable type (1234)*		Mongol invasions	Magna Carta (1215) Marco Polo (1254–1324)
	Completion of Tripitaka (1251)	YÜAN (1279–)		
1300	*Decline of Buddhism–Rise of Confucianism* *Beginning of punch'ŏng and white porcelain*	*uang Kung-wang* *Wu Chen, Ni Tsan and Wang Meng*		
	YI (1392–) Capital moved to Seoul (1394)	MING (1368–)	MUROMACHI or ASHIKAGA (1392–)	
1400	*Opening of Printing Burea (1403)* *Opening of Painting Bureau* King Sejong's "Hangŭl" (1443) *Discovery of cobalt at Sunch'ŏn and first official reference to blue-and-white porcelain made in Korea (1464)* *K ean Che School of Painting*	Naval expeditions of Admiral Cheng Ho (1405–1433) *Wu School of Painting* *Che School of Painting*		RENAISSANCE *Gutenberg's Press (ca. 1445)* Vasco da Gama's voyage around Cape of Good Hope to India (1497–1499) Magellan's voyage (1519–1522)
1500		Portuguese in Canton (1517)	*Sesshū (1420–1506)* First Europeans (Portuguese) in Japan (ca. 1542, introduction of firearms and Christianity; arrival of Jesuit Francis Xavier (1549) MOMOYAMA (1573–) *Karatsu* *Hagi*	*Sistine Chapel*
1600	Hideyoshi's invasion (1592–1598) First Manchu invasion (1627) Second Manchu invasion (1636)		EDO or TOKUGAWA (1615–) *Ukiyo-e* Exclusion Policy limiting foreign trade and contact (1633–1639)	BAROQUE PERIOD Establishment of English, Dutch and French East India Companies *Rembrandt (1606–1669)*
1700	"True landscape" movement in painting Genre painting *Introduction of Christianit (1777)* "Practical Learning" movement	CH'ING (1644–) *Foundation of College of Inscriptions (1677)* *Ts'ang Ying-hsüan appointed Supervisor at Ching-te chen (1682)* *Edition of 24 Standard Histories (1739–1766)* *General Catalogue of Ssu K'u Ch'üan (1789)*		American Independence (1776) French Revolution (1789–1793)
1800	"Beginning of direct Western influence *Closing of official Punwŏn kiln (1884)*			IMPRESSIONISM and POST IMPRESSIONISM
			MEIJI (1868–)	
		T'ai P'ing rebellion (1850–1864) Sino-Japanese War (1894–1895)		
1900	King Kojong takes the Imperial title (1897) Annexation by Japan (1910) Republic of Korea (1945–)	Republic of China (1912)	TAISHŌ (1912–) SHOWA (1926–)	

CATALOGUE

I

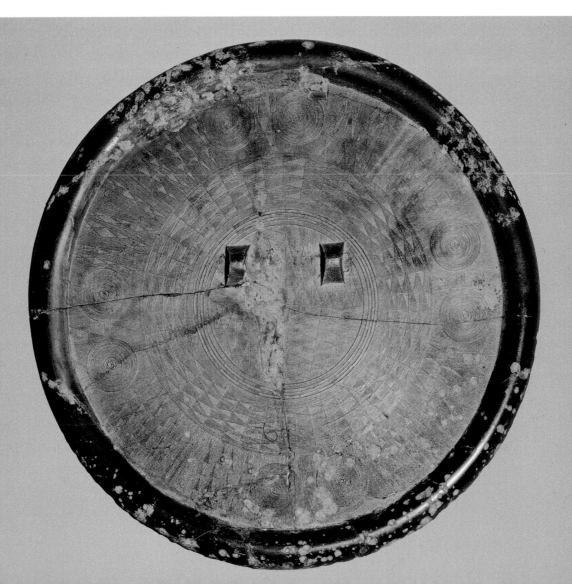

II

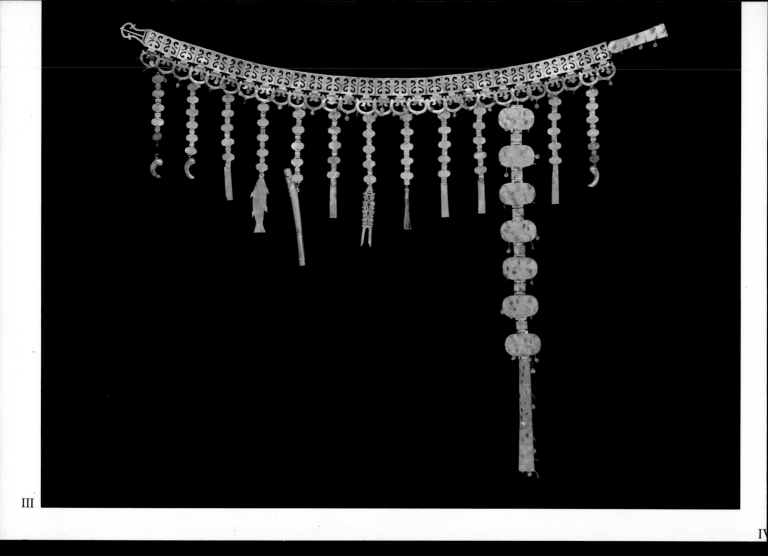

III

IV

V

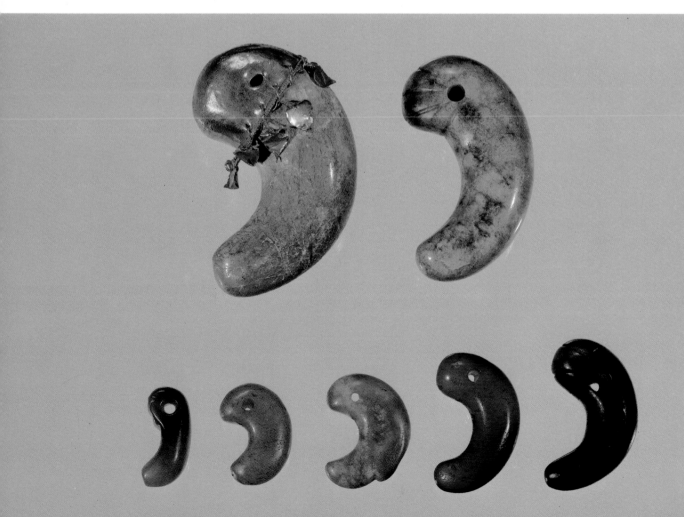

VI

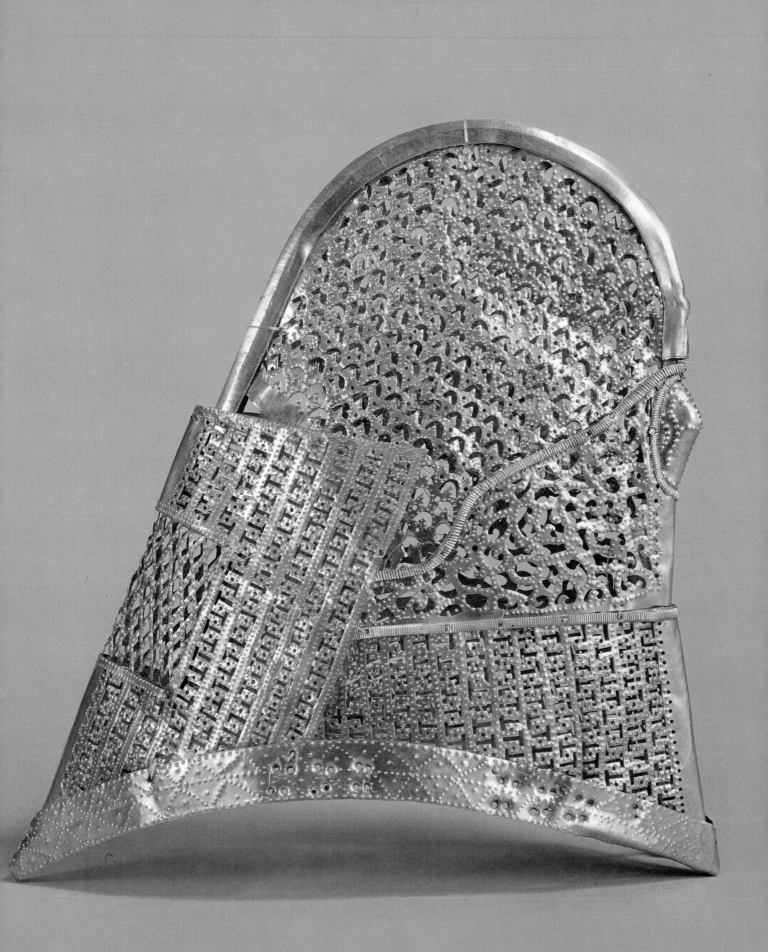

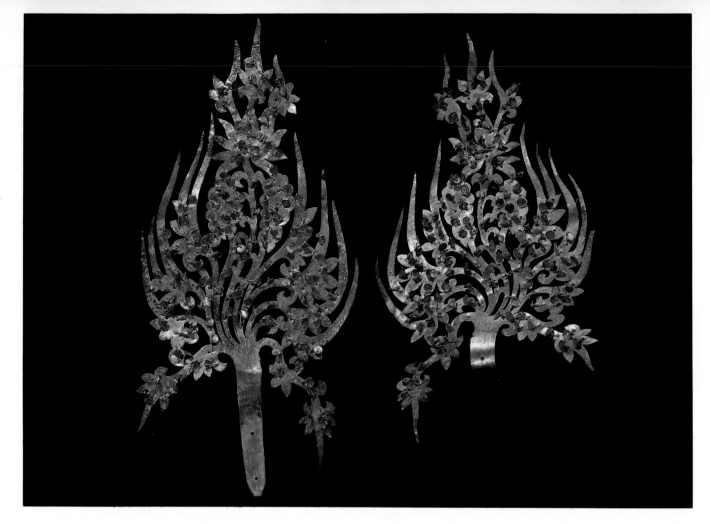

IX

X

XII

XIII

XIV

XXIX

XVII

XXXVIII

清�æ·±

XXXIX

X

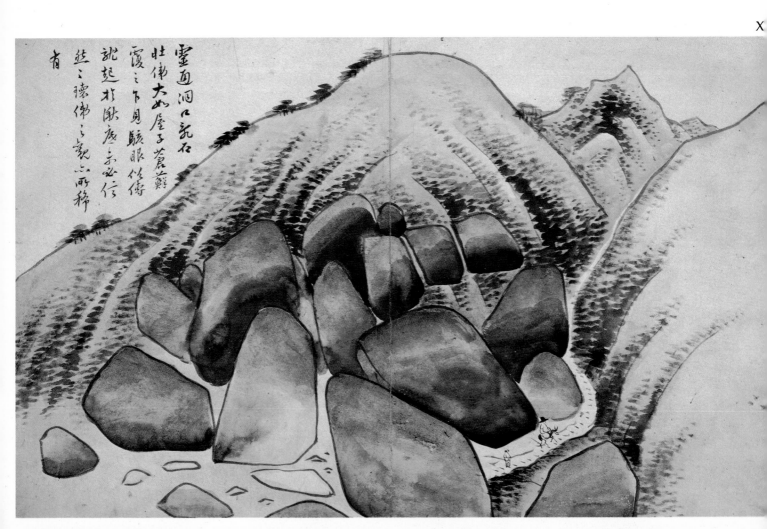

靈通洞口亂石
壯偉大如屋子蒼蘚
覆之不見頭眼修傳
說起非獄底未必信
兹之標佛之觀亦所稱
有

INTRODUCTION

PREHISTORY

Paleolithic sites, some probably dating as far back as 20,000 or 30,000 years ago, if not earlier, have been discovered in various parts of Korea during the past fifteen years or so. Important as they are, such findings have so far revealed nothing about the ethnic characteristics or living habits of these earliest occupants of the peninsula. We can only surmise that they lived strictly from hunting, fishing and fruit gathering.

Some 5,000 years ago, at the beginning of the revolutionary *Neolithic period*, a number of major technological changes took place in Korea as well as elsewhere in East Asia. The inhabitants of the peninsula gradually learned to make better stone tools and weapons, till the land and produce a low-fired "comb pattern" pottery which may be a variant of north Asian prototypes (No. 1). These people usually settled on river banks and built small villages of semi-subterranean pit houses with central fireplaces.

Plain Coarse Pottery period is the name given by archaeologists to a cultural stage which, from ca. 1000 to about 300 B.C., corresponds to the last phase of the neolithic period. In addition to simple but technically more advanced types of earthenware, this culture produced highly refined stone implements.

Following a succession of spectacular discoveries made during the past decade, it is now believed that *bronze metallurgy* was introduced at least as early as 600 B.C. (Nos. 2–7). This major technical revolution was accompanied by new burial practices necessitating the construction of monuments built with large stones and bearing strong resemblance to the megaliths of Western Europe and particularly Brittany: dolmens, cists, cairns, etc. (Fig. 1). Several of the objects selected for this exhibition were found in cists, i.e., graves lined with stone slabs (Nos. 2,3 and 4). The predilection shown by builders of royal tombs of the early historical period for large blocks of stone may have found its root in this megalithic past.

The earliest iron artifacts discovered so far are associated with a new type of pottery which is best exemplified by the so-called Kimhae culture in today's South Kyŏngsang

Figure 1: *Prehistoric dolmen from Unsŏng-ni, Ŭnyul-kun, Hwanghae Province.*

Province. It is, however, unlikely that this culture which developed during the 3rd or 2nd century B.C. corresponds to a true *Iron Age*, since bronze was obviously still widely in use until at least the 1st century B.C. (Colorplate II and Nos. 8–11).

The successive cultural changes and remarkable achievements of the prehistoric period have long captured the attention of Korean scholars. According to a current theory, the people of the Plain Coarse Pottery period originally migrated from the north. Known as Yemaek in modern Korean and probably of Tungusic stock, they brought with them the language which developed into present-day Korean.

Historians also like to evoke a myth recorded as far back as the 12th century A.D. in which Tan'gun, the founder of the first— and still legendary—kingdom of Korea, Chosŏn, was the son of a female bear and a Yemaek, himself the son of the divine creator. Be that as it may, the Korean people of today associate the birth of their nation with that of Tan'gun, which is traditionally placed in 2333 B.C. In the current dearth of archaeological data regarding prehistorical Korea, such theories and legends present at least the advantage of emphasizing that the unusually strong indigenous traits of the country as a cultural entity should not be ascribed to mere historical accidents.

THE HISTORICAL PERIOD

THE THREE KINGDOMS PERIOD (1st century B.C.–7th century A.D.)

Korean history proper begins at the very end of the second century B.C. when Han China invaded and occupied a sizeable territory in the northern part of the country in order to break an alliance between Chosŏn and the Huns. China was to maintain the flourishing colony of Lo-lang (Nangnang in Korean), north of the Han river, until 313 A.D.

Meanwhile, the ancestors of today's Koreans established several independent and rival states in the rest of the country.

Three of these states, Koguryŏ, Paekche, and Silla, dominated the political and cultural scene from the middle of the 1st century B.C. to the latter part of the 7th century A.D. This long formative period in the history of Korea is known as the Three Kingdoms period.

Koguryŏ (37 B.C.–668 A.D.) was by far the largest of the three, since it occupied a territory extending into Manchuria in the north and reaching the upper basin of the Han river in the south (Map No. 1). Because of its Manchurian origins and the proximity of Lo-lang until the beginning of the 4th century, Koguryŏ became increasingly receptive to Chinese political, economic, religious and artistic concepts. In fact, one of the main contributions of this otherwise bellicose state was the introduction of Buddhism into the peninsula as early as the late 4th century A.D. The offical date retained by historians is that of 372 A.D., when a monk named Sundo arrived in Koguryŏ from China bringing with him Buddhist scriptures and images (see Nos. 69 and 71 for Buddhist statuettes of Koguryŏ provenance). The importance of this visit can hardly be overemphasized, since Buddhism became rapidly a majo source of artistic inspiration from one end of the peninsula t the other (Nos. 69–80). The art of Koguryŏ is also well know for murals inspired by Chinese mythology and ancestor wor ship. The best of these remarkable wall paintings decorat tombs located in today's Manchuria.

To survive under the constant pressures exerted by it mighty neighbor in the north, the relatively small kingdom o Paekche (18 B.C.–660 A.D.) had to make the best of it privileged geographical situation. Located in the southwest ern part of the peninsula, it managed to maintain a clos relationship with Japan on the one hand and the Chines states of the lower Yangtze on the other. As a matter of fact Buddhism was not introduced into Paekche from the north bu from the southern Chinese state of Eastern Chin (317–42 A.D.) at a date corresponding to 384 A.D. The southern origi of Paekche Buddhism largely accounts for the marked stylisti features of many of the statuettes produced in the kingdom during the 6th and 7th centuries (Nos. 70, 73 and probably 75 76 and Colorplate XI as well). Paekche styles were in tur introduced into Japan by the second quarter of the sixth cen tury and constituted one of the major elements in the devel opment of the early schools of Japanese sculpture.

Furthermore, largely dependent as they were on souther Chinese models, the potters of this small but highly creativ state developed distinctive styles in vessels as well as in tom or temple tiles (Nos. 60–68).

Silla (57 B.C.–668 A.D.), the third of the Three Kingdoms counterbalanced Paekche in the southeast of the peninsula. It relatively isolated situation, the wealth of its ores, the in genuity of its craftsmen and its attachment to ancient tra ditions and religious beliefs are the major factors which con tributed to its highly original culture. The goldsmiths of Sill were not only among the most skillful in Asia; they also wer extraordinarily imaginative. Their crowns, girdles, necklaces bracelets and earrings are unique creations that have no rea counterparts anywhere in the Far East. Silla potters, too, pro duced many unusual shapes, some of which were adopted b Japanese potters of the Old Tombs period (3rd–6th centur A.D.). Jars with human and animal figurines (Nos. 39 and 43) stands or receptacles with tall perforated feet (Nos. 40–42) anthropomorphic or zoomorphic vessels (Frontispiec Colorplate VIII, and Nos. 44, 45, 49 and 50) and vessels in th shape of houses, boats or carts (Nos. 46–48) are among th most distinctive of this remarkable production. The Sill people were also great masons. Unlike those of Koguryŏ o

Paekche, the impressive mound tombs which they built for their rulers were made of stones disposed in such a manner that their inner chambers were practically inviolable. Quite a few of the most spectacular objects displayed in this exhibition remained in such tombs until the archaeological campaigns of recent years (see for instance Cover and Colorplates IV–VIII and Nos. 2–38, 44–46, and 48).

Silla resisted Buddhism for about a hundred and fifty years after it had been introduced everywhere else in Korea. In 527 A.D., however, Buddhism was officially accepted and quickly became a major source of artistic inspiration. The well known Pulguk-sa, the oldest surviving temple in Korea, dates from that period, since it was first built in 535 A.D. Latecomers as

as Kaya, located in the southern tip of the country and more or less controlled by Japan since the 4th century (Nos. 52–54). For the first time Korea was placed under a single dynastic rule known as Unified or Great Silla.

UNIFIED SILLA (668–935 A.D.)

Blessed with internal as well as eternal peace, the first century and a half after unification was one of the most flourishing periods in Korean history. Great progress was made in artistic and scientific fields. In 647, a few years prior to the unification of the country, the Silla rulers had erected the oldest observatory in the Far East—part of the structure can still be seen in Kyŏngju (Fig. 2). In 682, less than fifteen years

Figure 2: A twenty-two feet high stone observatory of Punae-myŏn, Kyŏngju, North Kyŏngsang Province, constructed in the 7th century, Silla Dynasty.

they were, Silla sculptors relied primarily on the "new" Chinese styles, those of the Northern Ch'i, Sui and early T'ang Dynasties (Colorplates XII–XIV and Nos. 77–81).

In the constant struggle for hegemony which marked the entire period of the Three Kingdoms, the odds were against Silla, but the astute rulers of this energetic state took advantage of the rise of the T'ang Dynasty early in the 7th century. They formed an alliance with this new imperial house which distrusted Koguryŏ and had no reason to favor Paekche. With the help of the T'ang army, Silla defeated Paekche in 660 A.D. and Koguryo in 668 A.D. About a century earlier (562 A.D.) Silla had absorbed a loose confederation of tiny states known

after uniting the country, they founded a university which, in addition to the complete cycle of Confucian studies, offered courses in medicine, mathematics, and astronomy.

Eager to catch up with Chinese technology and know-how, Unified Silla studied carefully the economic and cultural policies of the T'ang court and attempted to adapt them to her own needs. This was an era of brisk trade with China and also one of feverish urban activity. Kyŏngju, the capital, was enlarged and in its heyday, with one million inhabitants, must have been one of the largest, best planned and most beautiful cities in the world. Many of the objects shown in this exhibition were discovered in the foundations or ruins of some of the numerous palaces and temples of Kyŏngju and more particularly from a site recently excavated, that of the Anap-chi pond (or Anap Pond), a unique man-made structure which adjoined a detached palace and contained three artificial islands (Colorplates XV–XVIII and Nos. 85, 86, 93, 94, 100, 101).

The Buddhist church continued to prosper throughout the period. By the beginning of the 8th century, the church had become such a driving force that in addition to building numerous temples and monasteries (Colorplates XIV–XVIII and Nos. 81, 83, 92, 95, 98, 99), which also served as centers of learning and medical care, it also caused entire granite mountains, such as the Namsan near Kyŏngju, and granite caves, such as the famous Sŏkkuram (see Fig. 3), to come to life

institutions of Chinese inspiration, such as a taxpaying free peasantry or a corps of salaried civil servants recruited by examinations open to everyone, and the indigenous social order, which, being based on birthright, was exclusively aristocratic and hereditary. The problem was compounded by the deterioration of the central authority. The last century and a half in the existence of Unified Silla was plagued by incessant bloody feuds between various branches of the royal family, unrest in the provinces and the emergence of independent states in various parts of the country. Wang Kŏn, the ruler of one of these states, Koryŏ (an abbreviation of Koguryŏ), accepted in 935 the surrender of the last and powerless king of Silla.

Figure 3: The main Buddha from the Sŏkkuram cave temple, Kyŏngju, construction of which began in 751 A.D., Unified Silla Dynasty.

with carved and free-standing effigies of The Enlightened One and other deities of Mahāyāna Buddhism (see for instance No. 89).

Unified Silla potters introduced many new shapes and decorative devices, some of which were inspired by Chinese models created mainly in Chekiang Province. During the 8th or early 9th centuries intentional glazing appeared for the first time, thus preparing the way for the remarkable achievements of the next period (Colorplate XIX, No. 102).

After such a promising start, Unified Silla was already showing signs of decline by the end of the 8th century. This decline, which paralleled that of the T'ang empire, was largely due to incompatibilities between the new, often egalitarian

KORYŎ (918–1392 A.D.)

Although Wang Kŏn's descendants managed to keep the dynastic title alive for 474 years, the Koryŏ period actually includes two very different eras; their dividing point coincides with the first Mongol invasions which took place during the third decade of the 13th century.

Prior to these invasions, for almost three centuries, Koryŏ enjoyed complete independence despite several severe Khitan raids in the late 10th century, a short-lived but full-fledged Jurchen invasion in the early 12th century, and, about a century later, the beginning of over two centuries of systematic attacks by Japanese pirates.

Internal stability lasted only three or four generations. Starting from the early 11th century a number of rival clans and military factions threatened the ruling house, and toward the end of the 12th century the real power had fallen into the hands of the Ch'oe family which, with its huge estates, its private army and its own administration, was in fact governing the country.

Nevertheless, these three centuries were marked by important social changes and spectacular artistic achievements.

Society was as stratified as before, and high official positions continued to be monopolized by members of the royal family, their relatives and allies. The three main classes—aristocrats, commoners and "lowborn"—kept to themselves. Since 958, however, the Chinese system of examinations had been officially adopted, thus allowing, at least theoretically, scholarship and talent to become a source of social promotion.

As had been traditionally the case in China for a thousand years or so, the political administration of Korea was now highly centralized. Practically all the people in power resided in the capital, Songdo (modern Kaesŏng) which was transformed into a little Ch'ang-an with palaces and temples of such dimensions and luxury that they greatly impressed the Sung envoys who visited the city periodically.

Wang Kŏn and most of his successors were fervent Buddhists. Under their patronage Buddhism became for all practical purposes the official religion. The church grew in strength and reached all social classes. Buddhist monasteries were major centers of learning and art, but only a small proportion of what was created at the time had been preserved (see Colorplate XX and, for instance, Nos. 104–109). There are at least two reasons for the paucity of early Koryŏ Buddhist paintings, sculptures and even cult objects. On the one hand, Sŏn (Ch'an in Chinese and Zen in Japanese) Buddhism, which was gaining in popularity, did not encourage the making of effigies, and on the other hand practically all early Koryŏ paintings whether religious or secular have long since been destroyed.

In the final analysis, the main artistic contribution of early Koryŏ was made in the field of ceramics. Starting from the late 10th century and continuing for about three hundred years, kilns located on the eastern seaboard of the peninsula and particularly in South Chŏlla Province (see Map 2) produced large quantities of one of the most refined types of ceramics ever made in East Asia or in the world for that matter. Until the middle of the 12th century, these celadons were either plain or decorated with subdued incised, stamped or molded designs. At an early stage this production was already greatly admired by Sung connoisseurs (see Nos. 111 and 129). Around 1150

A.D. these traditional decorative techniques were supplemented with innovative and typically indigenous ones including inlay and underglaze painting (Nos. 120 and 154).

Koryŏ celadons attracted the attention of European and American connoisseurs early in this century and are, as of today, probably better known in the West than any other facet of Korean art. The bulk of the production consists of receptacles for the table and the writer's desk, or of flower vases. The first category, by far the largest, comprises bowls, cups, and small dishes (Nos. 112, 113, 115, 120, 123, 126, 131, 139, 144), as well as a variety of wine pots and bottles (Colorplates XXV–XXVII and Nos. 114, 116, 117, 122, 134, 140, 141). The second category consists essentially of water-droppers (Nos. 124, 125), and the third of tall, high-shouldered, small-mouthed vases made especially to hold plum blossoms (Colorplate XXVII and Nos. 121, 135, 136, 137, 138, 143). This list, however, is by no means complete. The same basic technique of applying celadon glazes to porcelaneous bodies was used for such diverse objects as incense burners (Colorplate XXVI and Nos. 118 and 129), pillows (Nos. 119 and 133), roof tiles (Nos. 127 and 128), water sprinklers used in Buddhist rituals (No. 130), toilet cases (No. 142), cosmetic boxes (No. 152), oil bottles (No. 153), etc.

Depending essentially on models found in the vegetable and animal kingdoms, shapes and ornamental schemes were at first straightforward and subdued. As time passed, however, they became increasingly elaborate. By the middle of the 12th century daring experiments were made that, in addition to inlaying, involved underglaze copper and iron decoration or even iron glazes (Colorplate XXVIII and Nos. 145–154). Only a few years ago such "painted" wares were automatically attributed to the 13th or even 14th century. A very active campaign of excavations conducted these past few years by the National Museum in the region of Puan and Kangjin (respectively in North and South Chŏlla Provinces) has revealed that several kilns in the region produced wares of these various types about a century earlier than was previously assumed.

Starting from 1231 Korea was repeatedly invaded and devastated by the same Mongol hordes who were about to establish the first foreign imperial dynasty in China. After putting up a gallant but ineffectual resistance, Koryŏ surrendered to the invaders in 1239, and for the next century or so the country was placed under Mongol rule. The powerless royal family became a branch of the Mongol ruling family through forced intermarriages, and Korea was made to participate in the unsuccessful expeditions staged against Japan by the Mongols in 1274 and 1281. The dynasty was too enfeebled to reassert itself even after the mighty Mongol empire collapsed in the middle of the 14th century. It became the easy prey of one of its generals who had been sent to southern Manchuria to support the retreating Mongols against the rising Ming Dynasty of China. This general, Yi Sŏng-gye, decided instead to overthrow the ruling house and to establish his own dynasty, a project which he brought to fruition in 1392.

Throughout this period of foreign domination and internal dissensions, the Buddhist church remained strong and active (Colorplates XXI–XXIII and Nos. 155–160). Wang Kŏn had placed the dynasty under Buddha's protection, and when his successors began to despair of being able to ward off the Mongol peril by sheer force, they turned to Buddha as their last hope. When the original printing blocks of the *Tripitaka* (the canonical scriptures of Buddhism) were destroyed by the Mongols, the court ordered a reimpression of this monumental work which necessitated the carving of 81,137 wooden blocks. Preserved today in a special building of the Haein-sa (*sa* being the Korean word for Buddhist monastery or temple) on Mt. Kaya, these blocks are the oldest ones of their kind in East Asia (see Fig. 4).

(Colorplates XXIII and No. 158). Unfortunately, only a handful of these works have survived the vicissitudes of the period.

The prestigious celadon kilns pursued their activities until the end of the dynasty, but with a notable decrease in quality and very little innovation. The creative urge of the former period had either dried up or was stifled by the new regime.

YI (1392–1910 A.D.)

Early Yi period (15th and 16th centuries)

Kingship never was a very vigorous institution in Korea, and the extraordinary longevity of the Yi Dynasty—it lasted five hundred and ten years—was due less to the strength of the dynastic line than to the necessity of maintaining the royal family on the throne as a national symbol in the face of adverse circumstances.

Yet Yi Sŏng-gye was a remarkable statesman whose energetic and imaginative policies set the stage for the entire period. His most far-reaching reforms included the establish-

Figure 4: View of the world's oldest set of Buddhist scriptures (Koryŏ Dynasty woodblocks completed in 1251), the Tripitaka Koreana, stored in Haein-sa, a temple located in the Kaya Mountains west of Taegu.

Some seventeen years before this huge collection of wooden blocks was completed (1251) a secular work had been printed by means of metallic movable types, an invention which preceded Gutenberg's own movable types by about 200 years.

A large number of Buddhist paintings were created during the latter part of the Koryŏ Dynasty, and Korean Buddhist painters of the time established an international reputation

ment of a new capital at Seoul, a land reform aimed at dislocating the huge estates constructed during the previous regime as well as at redistributing the lands to a wider group of government officials, the creation of highly privileged categories of subjects and a reorganization of the central and local governments based on the Chinese pattern.

In addition, Yi Sŏng-gye encouraged the rise of Confucianism and took measures to accelerate the fall of the

Buddhist Church, thus endorsing a trend that was already manifest towards the end of the Koryŏ period. The examination system was perfected but continued to be limited to the highest class of a still very stratified society.

As early as the 16th century the instruments of power and the organs of government were divided among factions, opposing families, private interests and at times generations, and, yet, the first two centuries of the new regime were replete with cultural and artistic achievements (Fig. 5). The Confucian curriculum produced a number of brilliant historians, geographers, philosophers, legalists, and linguists. Movable type was used extensively in ambitious projects placed, since 1403, under the responsibility of a Printing Bureau, and King Sejong (1419–1450), probably the most enlightened of all Yi rulers, developed a revolutionary phonetic system. Consisting of only twenty-eight simple and elegant signs and known as *hangŭl* (literally "Korean letters"), the system permitted people to write in Korean for the first time. Until then all writing had been done in Chinese, and the practice of using Chinese in scientific and official literature and correspondence was not discontinued until the beginning of this century. Since 1945, however, *hangŭl* has become the primary method of writing and has proven to be perfectly adaptable to modern Korean.

The major artistic contributions of early Yi, or of the entire period for that matter, are to be found in the fields of painting and ceramics.

A few excellent Buddhist paintings have survived from the 15th and possibly early 16th centuries, but the bulk of what has been preserved from that period is secular in nature.

Tohwasŏ or "Painting Bureau" was created early in the 15th century and consisted of professional artists, whose responsibilities included painting ancestral protraits such as No. 193, and, starting from the latter half of the 15th century, possibly also at times decorating porcelains made for the court (Colorplates XXX and XXXII and Nos. 171–175 or again 202–205 for the 18th century).

The landscapes, animals, plants and scholars in landscape settings which form the bulk of our selection for the 15th and 16th centuries were not produced by salaried professionals but by scholars who, while being highly proficient artists, painted exclusively for themselves and their friends on an amateur basis.

At first (15th century) Yi Dynasty painters, especially landscapists, were strongly influenced by the great Northern Sung tradition of China (Nos. 181 and 185). Very soon, however, the so called "Li-Kuo" manner (see No. 181) was modified or superseded by works reflecting the influence of the contemporary Che School of Ming China (Nos. 186 and 187) which itself had evolved from the Southern Sung tradition. In China the Che School smacked of professionalism but, living in an entirely different context, the amateur painters of Korea could afford to be very eclectic and to choose their models according to their own taste, regardless of affiliation to one Chinese school or another. Thus animal painting of the period generally belongs to the Southern Sung-Che School tradition (Nos. 182–184), whereas bamboo painting is reminiscent of Northern Sung prototypes (Nos. 188 and 189).

If dependence on Chinese concepts and techniques remained very strong throughout this early stage, some of the most original painters developed traits or idiosyncrasies that are definitely Korean. A certain vigorous humor served by unusually bold calligraphic statements and chromatic contrasts, a strong emphasis on verticality as opposed to depth and also, perhaps, a pronounced preference for silk are among the most noticeable of these indigenous characteristics.

Judging from records going back to King Sejong's reign, the output of early Yi kilns must have been considerable, for 321 (or 324 by another count) such kilns were officially listed. Unfortunately, only a very small portion of this production has been preserved intact.

Early Yi ceramics are not noted for delicate shapes, subtle glazes, minute ornamental schemes or elaborate decorative techniques. Generally robust, heavily potted and boldly decorated with great flourishes of the carving tool or painting hand, they offer a vivid contrast with the celadons of 12th and 13th centuries Koryŏ. Historians have rightly emphasized that there was no real break in continuity, and that early 15th century wares such as Nos. 163 and 164 were in direct line of descent from Koryŏ celadons. Yet the typical early Yi stoneware or porcelain reveals an entirely new masculine taste and a major departure from the past. So far as ornamental schemes and decorative techniques are concerned, the goldsmith's approach which had been so characteristic of Koryŏ ceramics, and which they might have inherited from the Silla tradition, is now replaced by the painter's approach. This very major step is but one aspect of the overwhelming process of sinicization that was taking place at the time. As a matter of fact Yi ceramics taken as a whole reflect, in their own way, the new aesthetics of Ming China.

Such generalities might give the impression that all early Yi ceramics were unsophisticated. This would be a simplistic and an erroneous impression. There were, in fact, two quite distinct categories of wares: the one, unpretentious, imaginative, made primarily for the people, and the other aristocratic and produced in government kilns for the court.

The first category, which was occasionally patronized by the government as well, consists of a variety of stonewares produced all over the country and designated by the generic term of *punch'ŏng* (see Colorplate XXIX and Nos. 163–167 and 176–180). These jars, bottles, flasks, bowls and dishes can be decorated by incision, stamping, sgraffito, or painting in iron oxide, but they all share two characteristics which are at the origin of their name: a white slip and a bluish green glaze. It is one of the ironies of history that this type of pottery contributed to the development of the celebrated tea ceremony wares of Japan, but did not, in Korea proper, really survive the devastating Japanese invasions of the late 16th century.

By contrast, a number of kilns controlled by a governmental agency specialized in the manufacture of white porcelain. Starting from the middle of the 15th century, this porcelain was frequently painted in underglaze blue in the best Chinese tradition but, as was the case in the field of painting, with a choice of motifs, compositions and brushstrokes that fre-

tory. The Japanese dictator Hideyoshi invaded the country twice, in 1592 and 1597, and just about thirty years later Korea was again devastated, this time by the Manchus who were about to take over China. In 1637 the country became a vassal state of the Ch'ing Dynasty, the new Chinese regime, and remained in that position until the end of the 19th century.

Throughout the 17th century the now well-established "Korean Che" School of painting made some rather timid attempts to experiment with Zen (Chinese: Ch'an; Korean: Sŏn) themes and concepts (Nos. 190, 191), and an elegant calligraphic style was developed by porcelain decorators working for official kilns (Colorplate XXXI and Nos. 198, 199). Otherwise this period was rather conservative.

Korea never quite recovered from the disastrous effects of the Japanese invasions, but, in spite of adverse social and political conditions, the 18th century was a period of renais-

Figure 5: Yi Dynasty pagoda of P'alsangjŏn built in 1624 at Pŏpju-sa, Poŭn-kun, North Ch'ungch'ŏng Province.

quently revealed an already well-established indigenous taste (Colorplate XXX and Nos. 168–175). Unlike *punch'ŏng* kilns which were scattered all over the country, most official kilns were located in the vicinity of Kwangju in South Chŏlla Province.

Late Yi period (17th – 20th centuries)

The last decade of the 16th and the first half of the 17th centuries correspond to a very somber chapter in Korean his-

sance in the arts and the humanities. Confucian scholarship and literature flourished under the relatively strong reigns of Yŏngjo (1724–1776) and Chŏngjo (1776–1800), and once again refreshing attitudes prevailed in the fields of painting.

Turning away from the strict "academic" Che tradition, imaginative landscapists like Chŏng Sŏn (Colorplate XXV and Nos. 219–221), Sim Sa-jŏng (No. 224), Yi In-sang (No. 225), Kang Se-hwang (Colorplates XXXIX–XL and No. 232), Kim Sŏksin (No. 233), Ch'oe Puk (Nos. 235–237) or even Yi In-mun

(Nos. 238 and 239) adopted the much more individualistic approach of the Chinese literati painters of the so-called Wu School. They never quite divorced themselves from Chinese traditions, but by choosing Korean scenery, the "true landscapes" of Chŏng Sŏn (see Colorplate XXXV and No. 219), and by animating their subjects with highly individualized calligraphic rhythms, they were able to create landscapes that are unmistakably Korean.

Another factor in the rejuvenation of Korean secular painting in the 18th century was the "discovery" of genre painting by such eminent artists as Kim Hong-do (Colorplate XXXVI and Nos. 228–229) and Sin Yun-bok (Colorplates XXXVII–XXXVIII and No. 230). This phenomenon is unique in the history of East Asian painting and can be explained in the light of the Korean brand of a special school of Confucian thought known as "Practical Learning" which flourished during the second part of the 18th century (see Colorplate XXXVI and No. 227). In any event, these delightful and colorful genre scenes are precious historical documents in addition to being visual delights. They furnish surprisingly detailed information on the manners and customs of all levels of society.

From the late 17th or early 18th centuries on, the talents of the best Korean potters seemed to have been almost exclusively channeled toward the costly production of white porcelains with underglaze painting mainly in blue, although iron brown and copper red are not unusual (Colorplates XXXI and XXXIII and Nos. 198, 201, 206–208 and 212). A few new shapes were introduced (Colorplate XXXII and No. 203) as were some elaborate ornamental schemes (Nos. 204, 205), but the bulk of the production remained faithful to the sturdy shapes and straightforward decoration of early Yi. In this age of great scholarly activity, a large number of accessories were made for the writer's desk (Colorplate XXXII and Nos. 202, 207, and 208).

The introduction of Western ideas through the spreading of Christianity and the beginning of direct commerce with the West took place in the late 18th and early 19th centuries. Until the end of the Yi such new ideas had very little cultural impact on a society noted for its extreme conservatism.

Until 1884, when they were definitely closed, the official Punwŏn kilns continued to produce white porcelain in the best 18th century tradition (Nos. 209–218). Some blue-and-white motifs reveal, however, a predilection for very abstract and frequently humorous renderings of traditional subjects (Nos. 215–217).

Nineteenth and early twentieth century painting was served by a few men of considerable talent. Some, such as Yi In-mun (Nos. 238, 239), Kim Tŭk-sin (No. 245), Yu Un-hong (No. 246) and Paek Ŭn-bae (No. 248), followed in the footsteps of Chŏng Sŏn, Kim Hong-do or Sin Yun-bok. Others, such as Kim Su-ch'ŏl (Nos. 243–244) and Hong Se-sŏp (No. 249), developed very personal styles without quite disengaging themselves from the 18th century tradition.

The same remarks apply to at least two of the three mid to late 20th century painters whose works constitute a fitting finale for this exhibition (Nos. 254 and 256).

COLORPLATE IDENTIFICATION

EARLY KOREA—NEOLITHIC, BRONZE AND IRON AGES (Ca. 3,000 B.C. - 1st Century B.C.)

1.   Jar (ca. 3,000 B.C.), Comb-Pattern pottery
3.   Jar (600–300 B.C.), black earthenware
2 a-k. Dagger, Arrowheads and Beads (600–300 B.C.), slate and jade

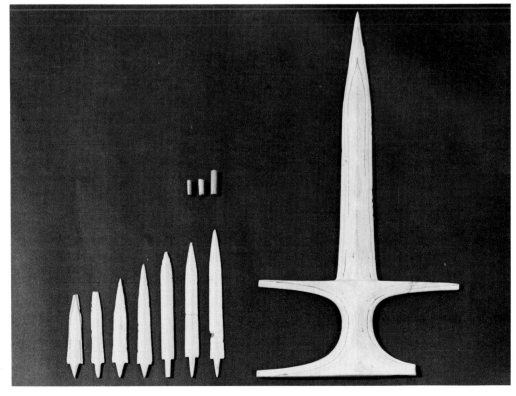

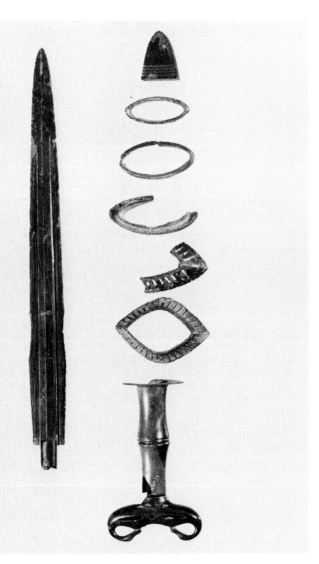

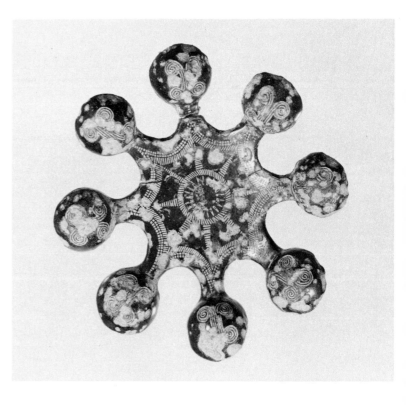

4a-c. Fittings (3rd–2nd century B.C.), bronze
7a-h. Sword and Fragments of Scabbard (3rd century B.C.), bronze
5. Rattle (3rd–2nd century B.C.), bronze

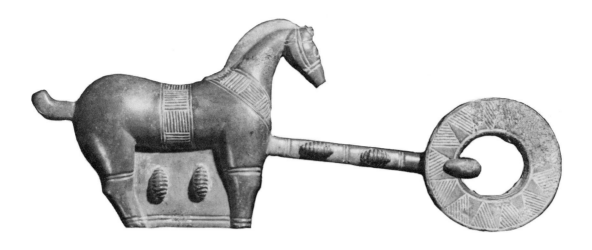

9-10. Belt Buckles (2nd–1st century B.C.), bronze
11.   Sword Pommel (1st century B.C.–1st century A.D.), bronze

Old Silla Jewelry and Metalwork (5th - 6th Centuries A.D.)

North Mound of Great Tomb at Hwangnam

12. Crown (ca. 5th century A.D.), gold and jade

13. Detail of Girdle (5th–6th century A.D.), gold and jade
14. Earrings (5th–6th century A.D.), gold
15. Bracelet (5th–6th century A.D.), gold

16a.   Cup (5th–6th century A.D.), gold
17a–b. Cups (5th–6th century A.D.), silver
18.   Bowl (5th–6th century A.D.), silver

19. Crown (5th–6th century A.D.), gold and jade

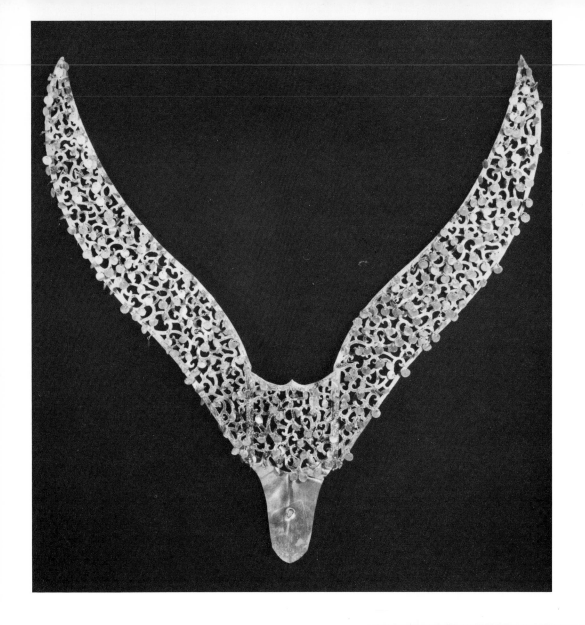

21. Cap Ornament (5th–6th century A.D.), gold
22. Ornament (5th–6th century A.D.), gold

66

Gold Bell Tomb

25. Necklace (5th–6th century A.D.), gold, jade and glass

Gold Crown Tomb

26. Tripod (*Chiao-tou*) (mid 6th century A.D.), bronze

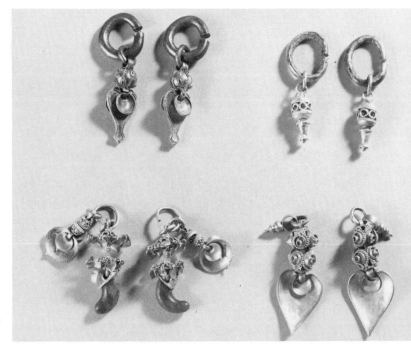

29.   Earrings (5th–6th century A.D.), gold
28.   Earrings (5th–6th century A.D.), gold and gilt bronze
30.   Earrings (5th–6th century A.D.), gold
27.   Crown Pendants (5th century A.D.), gold, jade and glass
31a–d. Earrings (5th–6th century A.D.), gold

31e–f and 32a–d. Earrings (5th–6th century A.D.), gold
33a–c. Pendants (5th–6th century A.D.), jade, gold and glass
34a.   Pendant (5th–6th century A.D.), jade and gold

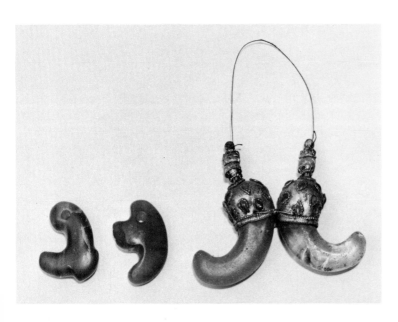

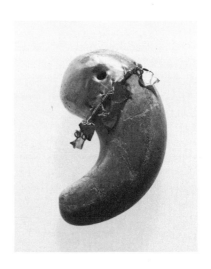

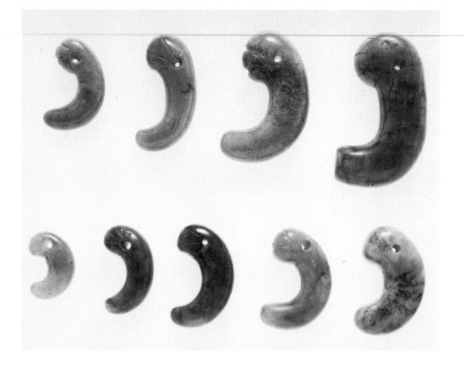

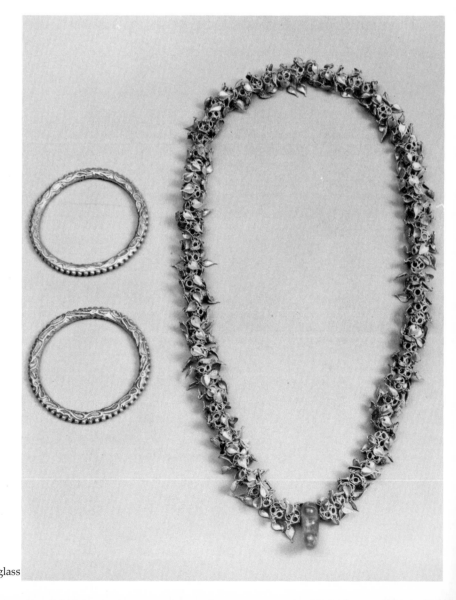

35a–i. Pendants (5th–6th century A.D.), jade
36. Pendant (5th century A.D.), glass
37a-b. and 38. Bracelets (5th-6th century A.D.), gold; and
  Necklace (5th-6th century A.D.), gold and glass

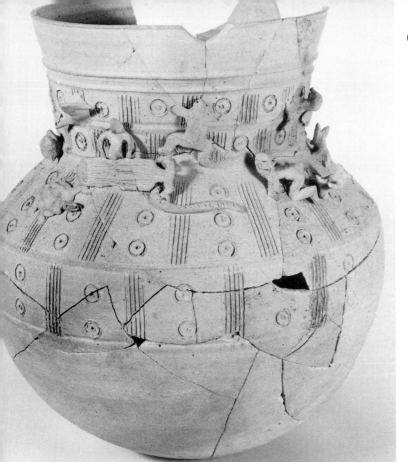

39. Jar (5th–6th century A.D.), stoneware
40. Jar (5th–6th century A.D.), stoneware

42. Stand for Jar (5th–6th century A.D.), stoneware
43. Jar with Deer (5th–6th century A.D.), stoneware
41. Stand for Jar (5th–6th century A.D.), stoneware

44. Dragon-Shaped Vessel (5th–6th century A.D.), stoneware
46a–b. Boat-Shaped Vessels (5th–6th century A.D.), stoneware

47.   Boat-Shaped Vessel (5th–6th century A.D.), stoneware
48.   Cart (5th–6th century A.D.), stoneware
49a–b. Cups with Horse Heads (5th–6th century A.D.), stoneware

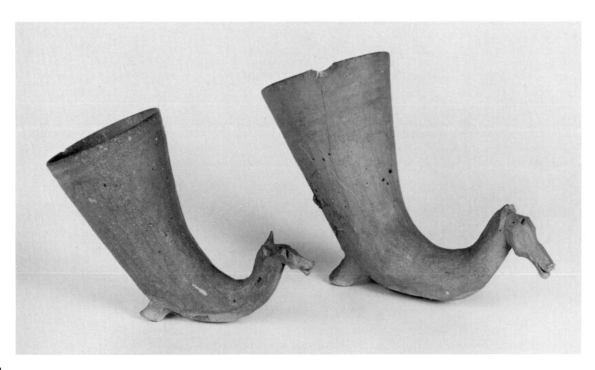

50–51. Horn-Shaped Cups with Horse and Boar
(5th–6th century A.D.), stoneware

Kaya Metalwork and Ceramics (5th-6th Centuries A.D.)

52.   Saddle Fitting (5th–6th century A.D.), gilt bronze

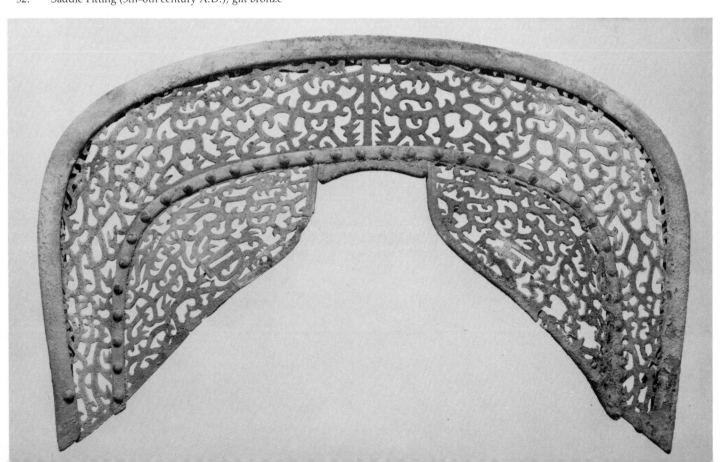

53a–b. Duck Shaped Vessels (5th–6th century A.D.), stoneware
54a–b. Chariot-Shaped Vessels (5th–6th century A.D.), stoneware

Paekche Jewelry, Metalwork, Sculpture and Ceramics (6th - 7th Centuries A.D.)
King Munyŏng's Tomb

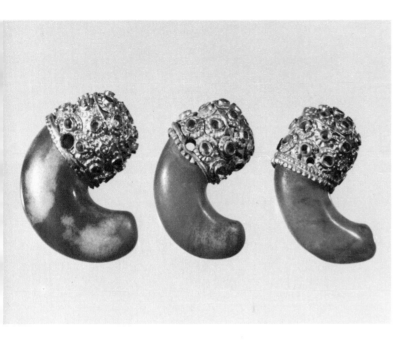

59a–c. Ornaments (early 6th century A.D.), jade and gold
58a–b. Queen's Bracelets (early 6th century A.D.), silver
60. Silver Cup with Bronze Stand (early 6th century A.D.)

61. Tomb Guardian (early 6th century A.D.), hornblende and iron
62a–b. Tomb Bricks (early 6th century A.D.), stoneware

63. Cup (6th–7th century A.D.), stoneware
64. Jar (6th–7th century A.D.), stoneware
65. Tile (early 7th century A.D.), earthenware

66–67. Tiles (early 7th century A.D.), earthenware
68a–c. Roof End-Tiles (7th century A.D.), stoneware

70. Buddhist Triad (dated 563 A.D.), gilt bronze
71. Buddha (late 6th century A.D.), gilt bronze
69. Buddha (probably 539 A.D.), gilt bronze

72. Buddha (late 6th century A.D.), gilt bronze
73. Buddha (late 6th century A.D.), steatite
74. Maitreya (6th century A.D.), gilt bronze
75. Maitreya (late 6th–early 7th century A.D.), gilt bronze

76. Maitreya (early 7th century A.D.), gilt bronze
78. Buddha (early 7th century A.D.), gilt bronze

80. Bodhisattva (mid 7th century A.D.), granite

UNIFIED SILLA (668 - 935 A.D.)
Buddhist Sculpture (7th - 9th Centuries A.D.)

82. Bhaiṣajyaguru (late 7th century A.D.), gilt bronze
83. Amitābha (ca. 706 A.D.), gold
84. Bhaisajyaguru (8th century A.D.), gilt bronze

86. Bodhisattva (8th century A.D.), gilt bronze
88. Bodhisattva (8th century A.D.), gilt bronze
87. Avalokiteśvara (early 8th century A.D.), gilt bronze

89. Head of Vajrāpaṇi (mid 8th century A.D.), granite
90. Zodiac Figure of Monkey (8th century A.D.), granite

92. Buddha (late 8th–early 9th century A.D.), cast iron

93. Dragon Heads (7th–8th century A.D.), gilt bronze and copper plate
94. Snuffers (7th–8th century A.D.), gilt bronze
95a–d. Gold Śarīra Casket, Glass Śarīra Bottle, Gold Sūtra Tablets
and Gold Case for Sūtra Tablets (8th century A.D.)

97–98. Roof End-Tiles (7th–8th century A.D.), stoneware
100.   Roof End-Tile (8th century A.D.), stoneware

99. Roof End-Tile (8th century A.D.), stoneware
101. Tile (8th century A.D.), stoneware
103. Funeral Urn (8th–9th century A.D.), stoneware

104.   Head of a Buddha (10th century A.D.), cast iron
105a–b. Shrine with Buddhist Triad (10th–11th century A.D.), gilt bronze

106. Kettle (10th–11th century A.D.), bronze
108. Miniature Pagoda (11th–12th century A.D.), bronze
107. Incense Burner (11th–12th century A.D.), gilt bronze

Ceramics (Late 11th-13th Centuries A.D.)

110.   Box (11th–12th century A.D.), silver-inlaid bronze

111–112. Vase and Wine Cup with Stand (early 12th century A.D.), incised celadon

113a–b. Dishes (early 12th century A.D.), celadon
115.　　Bowl (late 11th–early 12th century A.D.), incised celadon
114.　　Wine Pot (early 12th century A.D.), incised celadon

119. Pillow (early 12th century A.D.), incised celadon with underglaze ire
120. Bowl (mid 12th century A.D.), inlaid and incised celadon
121. Maebyŏng (1st half, 12th century A.D.), incised celadon

122. Bottle (1st half, 12th century A.D.), incised celadon
123. Bowl (1st half, 12th century A.D.), carved and incised celadon

126. Bowl (12th century A.D.), incised and inlaid celadon
125. Monkey-and-Baby-Shaped Water-Dropper (1st half, 12th century A.D.), celadon with underglaze iron
124. Duck-Shaped Water-Dropper (1st half, 12th century A.D.), celadon with underglaze iron

127 and 128a–b. Roof End-Tiles (early 12th century A.D.), celadon

130. Kuṇḍikā (mid 12th century A.D.), inlaid celadon
129. Incense Burner (12th century A.D.), incised celadon with underglaze iron
131. Bowl (mid 12th century A.D.), inlaid celadon

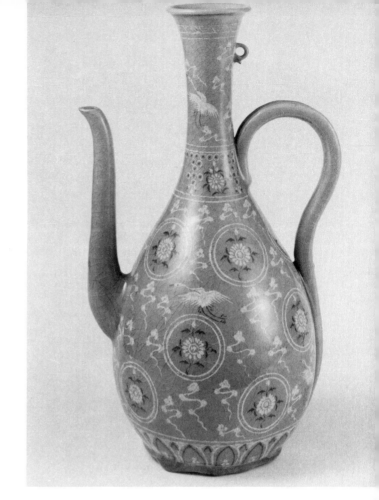

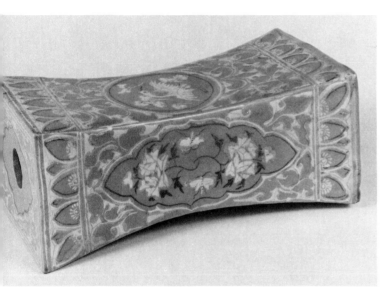

134. Wine Pot (mid 12th century A.D.), inlaid celadon
133. Pillow (mid 12th century A.D.), inlaid celadon
132. Jar (mid 12th century A.D.), inlaid celadon

135. Maebyŏng (mid 12th century A.D.), inlaid celadon

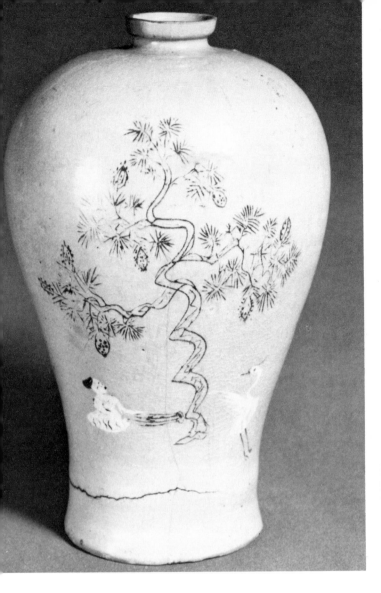

138. Maebyŏng (mid 12th century A.D.), inlaid celadon
137. Maebyŏng (mid 12th century A.D.), inlaid celadon
    with underglaze copper

141. Wine Pot (mid 12th century A.D.), inlaid celadon
140. Wine Pot (mid 12th century A.D.), incised and inlaid celadon
139. Cup (mid 12th century A.D.), inlaid celadon

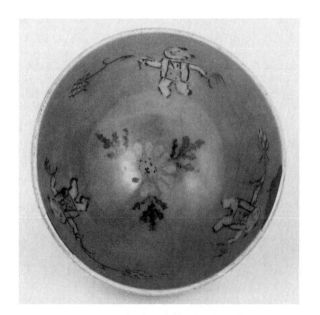

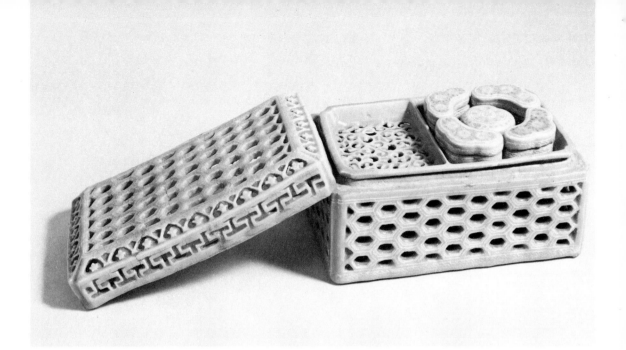

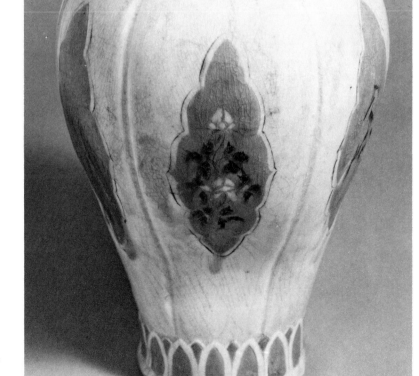

142. Toilet Case (mid–late 12th century A.D.), inlaid
      and openworked celadon
144. Bowl (mid 12th century A.D.), marble ware
143. Maebyŏng (mid 12th century A.D.), celadon-inlaid white ware

145. Cup with Stand (mid 12th century A.D.), porcelaneous ware with underglaze copper
146. Maebyŏng (mid 12th century A.D.), iron-glazed ware with underglaze iron
147. Maebyŏng (12th century A.D.), iron-glazed ware with underglaze iron
148. Covered Bowl (12th century A.D.), iron-glazed ware with underglaze iron

151. Bowl (13th century A.D.), inlaid celadon
150. Wine Pot (12th century A.D.), celadon with slip and underglaze iron

152. Cosmetic Box (late 12th century A.D.), celadon
    with slip, underglaze iron and copper
153. Oil Bottle (13th century A.D.), inlaid celadon
154. Vase (late 12th century A.D.), iron-glazed ware
    with reverse inlay

155. Banner Staff with Dragon Head (12th–13th century A.D.), bronze

159.   Buddhist Vessel (14th century A.D.), bronze
160.   Covered Bowl (14th–15th century A.D.), bronze
161–162. Masks (918-1392 A.D.), painted wood

YI (1392 - 1910 A.D.)
Ceramics (15th - 16th Centuries A.D.)

163. Placenta Jar (15th century A.D.), *punch'ŏng* stoneware
164. Bowl (15th century A.D.), *punch'ŏng* stoneware

167. Bottle (15th century A.D.), *punch'ǒng* stoneware
170. Bottle (early 15th century A.D.), iron-inlaid white porcelain
169. Bowl (15th century A.D.), iron-inlaid white porcelain

168. Covered Bowl (15th century A.D.), incised white porcelain
171. Maebyŏng (dated 1489 A.D.), blue-and-white porcelain

172. Jar (15th century A.D.), blue-and-white porcelain
174. Water-Dropper (15th century A.D.), blue-and-white porcelain

175. Jar (16th century A.D.), white porcelain with underglaze iron

176. Flask (16th century A.D.), *punch'ŏng* stoneware
178. Bottle (16th century A.D.), *punch'ŏng* stoneware
177. Jar (16th century A.D.), *punch'ŏng* stoneware

179. Jar (16th century A.D.), *punch'ŏng* stoneware
180. Bottle (16th century A.D.), *punch'ŏng* stoneware

181a–d. *Landscapes*, attributed to An Kyŏn (born 1418 A.D.)

182. *Four Goats*, Anonymous, (15th–16th century A.D.)
183. *A Dog and Puppies*, by Yi Am (died after 1545 A.D.)

A Bull, by Kim Che (born after 1509 A.D.)
185a–b. *Landscapes,* by Hoeŭn (ca. 16th century A.D.)

186. *Landscape*, attributed to Yi Kyŏng-yun (born 1545 A.D.)
187a–b. *A Scholar Washing His Feet* and *Two Scholars Conversing About Wild Geese*, attributed to Yi Kyŏng-yun (born 1545 A.D.)

188. *Bamboo in the Wind,* by Yi Chŏng (died 1622 A.D.)
189. *Bamboo,* by Yi Chŏng (died 1622 A.D.)

190a–b. *Autumn Moon Over Tung-t'ing Lake* and *Night Rain on the Hsiao and Hsiang Rivers,* attributed to Kim Myŏng-guk (died after 1662 A.D.)

191a–b. *A Strolling Scholar* and *A Gentleman on a Donkey,* by Kim Myŏng-guk (died after 1662 A.D.)

192a–c. *Landscapes,* by Yun Ŭi-rip (died 1643 A.D.)

193. *Portrait of Yi Hang-bok*, Anonymous (early 17th century A.D.)
195. *A Swimming Duck*, Anonymous (ca. 17th century A.D.)

197. *Hens and Chickens,* by Pyŏn Sang-byŏk (18th century A.D.)
196. *Cats and Sparrows,* by Pyŏn Sang-byŏk (18th century A.D.)

199. Bottle (late 17th century A.D.), blue-and-white porcelain
202. Brush Stand (18th century A.D.), blue-and-white porcelain

201. Bottle (17th–18th century A.D.), white porcelain with underglaze blue, copper and iron
205. Vase (mid 18th century A.D.), blue-and-white porcelain
204. Jar (18th century A.D.), blue-and-white porcelain

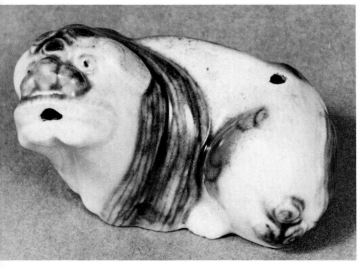

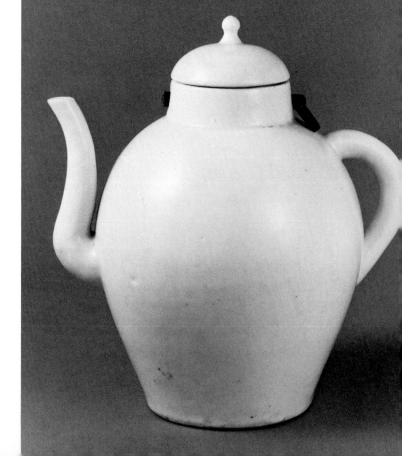

206. Jar (18th century A.D.), porcelain with underglaze copper
207. Water-Dropper (18th century A.D.), blue-and-white porcelain with underglaze copper
209. Pitcher (19th century A.D.), white porcelain

210. Water-Dropper (19th century A.D.), white porcelain
211. Brush Stand (19th century A.D.), white porcelain
212. Water-Dropper (19th century A.D.), white porcelain with underglaze copper
214. Water-Dropper (early 19th century A.D.), blue-and-white porcelain
213. Bowl (19th century A.D.), blue-and-white porcelain

131

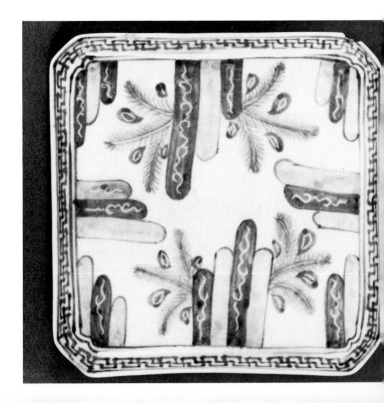

218. Water-Dropper (19th century A.D.), blue-and-white porcelain
216. Dish (19th century A.D.), blue-and-white porcelain
215. Dish (19th century A.D.), blue-and-white porcelain
217. Dish (19th century A.D.), blue-and-white porcelain

Painting (18th - 20th Centuries A.D.)

220. *Clear Skies Over Mount Inwang,* by Chŏng Sŏn (dated 1751 A.D.)
221. *Greeting Japanese Envoys in Tongnae,* (Overall and Detail), attributed to Chŏng Sŏn (died 1759 A.D.)

223. *Portrait of Yi Chae,* Anonymous (probably 18th century A.D.)
222. *A Dog Scratching,* by Kim Tu-ryang (died 1763 A.D.)

224. *Looking for Plum Blossoms*, by Sim Sa-jŏng (dated 1766 A.D.)
225. *Viewing the Waterfall*, by Yi In-sang (died 1760 A.D.)

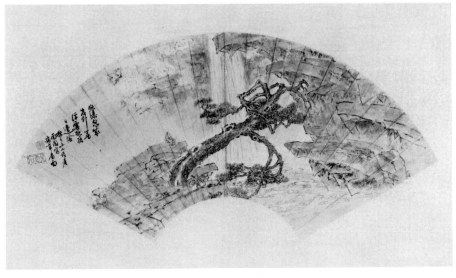

終人花鹿黄金
韻七樹
莉村丁度居
花主提
揭
稻崖若嫻和
雨绂
人重文都神

226. *Listening to a Golden Oriole,* by Kim Hong-do (died after 1814 A.D.)
228a. *Wrestling Match,* by Kim Hong-do (died after 1814 A.D.)

227a–b. *Immortal and Crane* and *Chatting on the Southern Mountain,* by Kim Hong-do (died after 1814 A.D.)

229. *Ceremonial Procession,* attributed to Kim Hong-do (died after 1814 A.D.)

230c,b,d. *Party by the Lotus Pond, Sword Dance,* and *Boating Excursion,* by Sin Yun-bok (born 1758 A.D.)

138

獰猛磨牙說逐純土東海
老黃公
于今跋扈橫行者誰識人中
此頰同
甲午南書

231. *A Tiger,* Anonymous (probably 18th century A.D.)
232a. *White Stone Pool* from *Scenic Spots of Songdo,* by Kang Se-hwang
       (died 1791 A.D.)

名石潭之
在靈通路
傍石白如雪
方如棊局
清流布之
上四山紫
翠紛滴金
時微雨下晴
景九色朦朧
不雜烏也

234. *A Plantain Tree and Rock,* by King Chǒngjo (died 1800 A.D.)

233. *Mount Tobong,* by Kim Sǒk-sin (born 1758 A.D.)

235. *A Strolling Old Scholar*, by Ch'oe Puk (active mid 18th century A.D.)

237. *Fishing on the River on a Spring Day*, by Ch'oe Puk (active mid 18th century A.D.)

236. *Returning Home on a Windy and Snowy Night*, by Ch'oe Puk (mid 18th century A.D.)

238. *Mountains and Rivers Without End* (Two Sections and Detail), by
Yi In-mun (died 1821 A.D.)

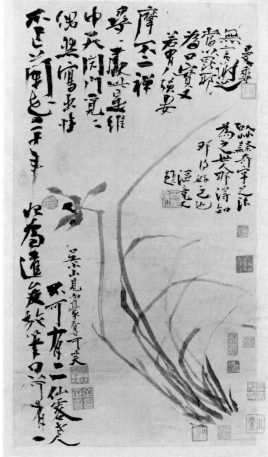

239. *A Gathering of Four Friends,* by Yi In-mun (dated 1820 A.D.)
240. *Orchids,* by Kim Chŏng-hŭi (died 1857 A.D.)

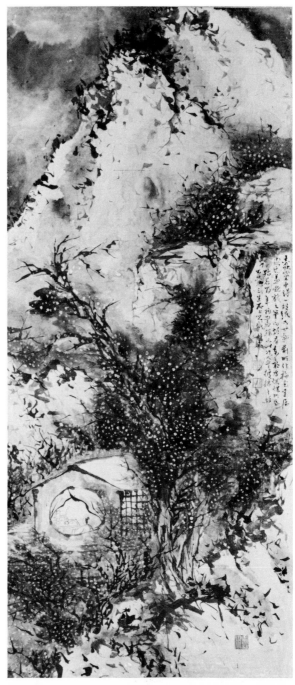

243. *Leisurely Conversation Under Pine Trees,* by Kim Su-ch'ŏl
(active mid 19th century A.D.)

241. *Plum Blossom Studio,* by Cho Hŭi-ryong (died 1859 A.D.)

144

242. *Butterflies*, by Cho Hǔi-ryong (died 1859 A.D.)
244a–b. *Flowers*, by Kim Su-ch'ǒl (active mid 19th century A.D.)

248. *Traveling along the Riverside,* by Paek Ŭn-bae (died after 1894 A.D.)
246. *Women,* by Yu Un-hong (died 1859 A.D.)
245. *Blacksmiths,* by Kim Tŭk-sin (died 1822 A.D.)

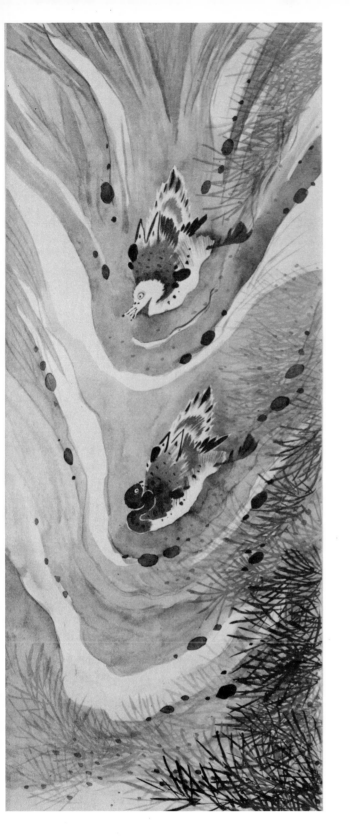

具足慧相觀寧官身是惟
丹青之咄咄逼真誰更知天
地弘絲羅心胸隨遇而神

茗山真
影

小塘寫

老驥題

249. *Swimming Ducks,* by Hong Se-sŏp (born 1831 A.D.)
247. *Portrait of Kang Yi-o,* by Yi Chae-gwan (died 1837 A.D.)

252. *Eagles,* by Chang Sŭng-ŏp (died 1897 A.D.)
251. *Homecoming,* by Chang Sŭng-ŏp (dated 1890 A.D.)
250. *A Gentleman Watching Geese,* by Chang Sŭng-ŏp (died 1897 A.D.)

254. *Elegant Gathering at Mount Tobong,* by Yi Yong-u (died 1952 A.D.)

253. *Visiting the Peach Blossom Spring,* by An Chung-sik (dated 1913 A.D.)

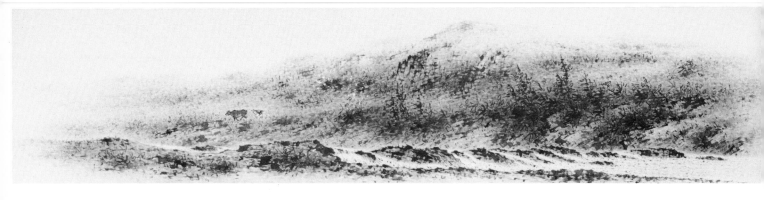

255. *Landscape*, by Yi Sang-bŏm (died 1972 A.D.)

256. *Autumn Colors on Samson Peak in the Diamond Mountains*, by Pyŏn Kwan-sik (dated 1959 A.D.)

ENTRIES

1. Jar   Comb-pattern pottery ware, earthenware
Neolithic (ca. 3,000 B.C.)
From Amsa-dong Seoul, Kyŏnggi Province
H. 53 cm
Sungjŏn University Museum

Originally found in fragmentary condition, this relatively thin-walled conical vessel is decorated from mouth to base with incised geometric designs. Four rows of fine, slightly curvilinear hatchings occupy the region of the mouth while the rest of the vessel is covered with a loose pattern of her-ringbones, also arranged in four rows.

Typical as they are of the so-called "comb-pattern pot-tery" of neolithic Korea, such shapes and ornamental schemes have also been discovered in the Volga river basin, southern Siberia and Japan. Their closest parallels may be found in early Jōmon pottery of the Sobata type.

Amsa-dong is located on the Han River, near Seoul.

2 a-k. Dagger, Seven Arrowheads, and Three Tubular Beads   Slate and jade
Bronze Age (600 B.C. - 300 B.C.)
From Mugye-ri, Kimhae, South Kyŏngsang Province
L. (Dagger) 46 cm; L. (Arrowheads) 11-18.8 cm; L. (Beads) 1.8-3 cm
National Museum of Korea

The dagger and arrowheads are made of such soft stone that they could never be put to any practical use. These were ceremonial weapons as corroborated by the unwieldly proportions of the dagger.

The Mugye-ri site, not far from Kimhae in the southeast-ern tip of the peninsula, is a cist which also yielded four bronze arrowheads and fragments of polished red pottery.

3. Jar   Black earthenware
Bronze Age (600 B.C. - 300 B.C.)
From Koejŏng-dong, Taejŏn, South Ch'ungch'ŏng Province
H. 22 cm
National Museum of Korea

In spite of its elegant proportions and relatively smooth con-tours, this bottle-shaped jar was most likely fashioned without the help of a wheel. It was found in a cist with various bronze artifacts and a vessel of plain red pottery.

The tomb was probably built for one of the Yemaek Tun-gus chieftains who brought bronze culture to the peninsula.

Recent excavations have uncovered several other fine examples of polished black pottery of the late Bronze and Iron Ages, the latter dating to the first few centuries A.D.

4 a-c. Three Fittings   Bronze
Late Bronze or Early Iron Age (3rd - 2nd century B.C.)
From Koejŏng-dong, Taejŏn and Namsong-ri, Asan, South Ch'ungch'ŏng Province
H. 25.4 cm, 22.3 cm and 22.1 cm (left to right)
National Museum of Korea

One side of these objects is convex and the other flat. Each section of the convex side is incised with two concentric bands, and each band consists of two fillets, the other one displaying fine striations and the inner one four parallel lines of hatchings. In addition, each section is equipped with a small torsaded ring connected to the body by means of a sturdy loop.

These objects have been compared to dagger handles or to sections of a bamboo stem split in half. It has been theorized that they were ornaments for the legs of horses or

again ritual implements worn by shamans or chieftains. All this must remain conjectural for the present.

With its cist (grave lined with stone slabs) covered by a cairn (rounded or pyramidal heap of stones), the Koejŏng-dong burial site is related to Bronze Age tombs in Liaoning Province in China and southern Siberia.

5. Rattle With Eight Jingle Bells   Bronze
Late Bronze or Early Iron Age (3rd - 2nd century B.C.)
From Taegong-ni, Hwasun, South Chŏlla Province
D. 12.3 cm
National Museum of Korea

The central post of this unusual instrument is decorated with a complex geometric motif made primarily of incised striations and hatchings, as was the case with the previous example (No. 4). On the other hand, the compounded spi-rals of Chinese origin that are incised on the jingle bells re-call those decorating the bronze finials (No. 6). These stylis-tic and technical analogies apply to objects found far apart in the southern half of the peninsula. Since all these objects are thought to have fulfilled some ceremonial function, probably inspired by shamanistic beliefs, they might indi-cate that the south of Bronze Age Korea was religiously and culturally more unified than is generally assumed.

It has been otherwise noted that many southern bronzes are original forms with strong religious connotations, where those of the north are more practical and reflect the influ-ence of prototypes developed in Manchuria and Liaoning.

6 a-b. Two Finials with Jingles   (See Colorplate I) Bronze
Late Bronze or Early Iron Age (3rd - 2nd century B.C.)
From Kangwŏn Province
H. 15.8 cm and 15.6 cm (left and right)
Kim Dong-hyon Collection

With their rows of incised striations and addorsed spirals, these finials present stylistic and technical affinities with the preceding rattle (No. 5) and fittings (No. 4). Bases are hol-low to allow for the insertion of handles probably made of wood. Tops are also partially hollow and contain a pellet that rattles when agitated.

Like the preceding bronze objects, these were probably used in religious ceremonies.

7 a-h. Short Sword with Handle and Six Fragments of Scabbard   Bronze
Late Bronze or Early Iron Age (3rd century B.C.)
From Pisan-dong, Taegu, North Kyŏngsang Province
L. (Dagger) 33.2 cm; L. (Handle) 12.5 cm
Hoam Art Museum

Such slender leaf-shaped, tanged weapons with a faceted median rib have been found all over Korea and are derived from Chinese models as they existed in the Liaotung penin-sula as early, at least, as the 6th century B.C.

The elegant handle with its bamboo-like stem and its two highly abstracted regardant birds may have been inspired by Steppe art prototypes. The body of the scabbard was made of a perishable material such as leather.

8. Mirror   (See Colorplate II)   Bronze
Early Iron Age (2nd - 1st century B.C.)
From Yongam, South Chŏlla Province
D. 21.2 cm
Sungjŏn University Museum

With its thick, plain rounded rim, its flat, thin body and its two loop handles, this object is typical of a small group of mirrors which were only remotely inspired by Chinese War-ring States' prototypes, and are regarded as the most sophisticated and original of all Bronze Age Korean mirrors.

Found in the southern part of the peninsula, but in provinces as far apart as South Chŏlla and Kangwŏn, these mirrors are consistently and densely decorated in extremely fine raised lines with geometric motifs based essentially on triangles, lozenges and concentric circles.

9-10. Two Belt Buckles in Shape of Horse and Tiger Bronze
Early Iron Age (2nd - 1st century B.C.)
From Ŏŭn-dong, Yongch'ŏn, North Kyŏngsang Province
L. (Horse) 18.6 cm.; (Tiger) 22.2 cm.
National Museum of Korea

The horse is in the round while the back of the tiger is flat. Despite this structural difference, the buckles are so similar in style and craftsmanship that they appear to be products of the same workshop.

They are related to northeast Asian and north Chinese prototypes, but display enough indigenous characteristics to be immediately distinguishable from all other buckles produced in those regions. Among the most striking of these characteristics are disproportionately large limbs, long, sturdy, tubular hooks and incised decorative motifs which, not unlike those of the preceding objects, consist mainly of striations, chevrons and hatchings.

The oval, shell-like ornaments that stand in high relief on the stem of the hook and under the horse's belly suggest three-dimensional objects found in association with the buckles, but the exact nature and function of these objects remain to be explained.

11. Sword Pommel   Bronze
Iron Age (1st century B.C. - 1st century A.D.)
From Yangdong-ni, Kimhae, South Kyŏngsang Province
L. 12 cm
Kang Su-yang Collection

The only one of its type discovered so far, this cruciform pommel is adorned with two pairs of diminutive, but very alert horses in the full round. Here again the Korean artist was able to naturalize with considerable virtuosity what was originally a north Chinese or northeast Asian theme.

It is interesting to note that this sword pommel was found in association with a late 1st century B.C. Chinese TLV mirror.

12. Crown with Pendants   Gold and jade
Old Silla (ca. 5th century A.D.)
From the North Mound of the Great Tomb at Hwangnam (Tomb No. 98), Kyŏngju, North Kyŏngsang Province
H. (Crown) 27.5 cm; L. (Longest Pendant) 30.3 cm
Kyŏngju National Museum

Excavated from a royal tomb in 1974, this is the most complete and elaborate of the five gold crowns so far discovered in Korea, all in the Kyŏngju area.

Three tree-shaped and two antler-shaped uprights which seem to reflect shamanistic beliefs or traditions project from a circular headband. From the same headband hang three pairs of pendants in the shape of elongated earrings. Each component is adorned with numerous comma-shaped pieces of jade and circular spangles which are attached by twisted gold wires. Like the rest of the crown, the spangles were cut from gold sheets.

Unknown in China, such crowns are thought to be derived from Siberian prototypes.

The Hwangnam-taech'ong sepulcher (or the Great Tomb at Hwangnam) is a twin tumulus of which the north mound is the tomb of a queen who may have been King Soji's queen. Korean archaeologists believe that King Soji was buried in the south mound in 502 A.D.

13. Girdle with Pendants   (See Colorplate II)
Gold and jade
Old Silla (5th - 6th century A.D.)

From the North Mound of the Great Tomb at Hwangnam (Tomb No. 98), Kyŏngju, North Kyŏngsang Province
L. (Girdle) 120 cm; (Longest Pendant) 77.5 cm
Kyŏngju National Museum

This royal gold sheet girdle consists of twenty-eight square openwork links hinged to as many heart-shaped rings from which hang, by means of twisted gold wires, thirteen articulated pendants made of oval elements alternating with square ones. Six of the pendants, including the largest one, end with plain, rectangular, tablet-like projections; another three display comma-shaped ornaments; and the remaining four support a variety of objects among which a fairly realistic fish, a pair of tweezers and a sheathed knife are easily recognizable. Spangles dangling from the upper rings and the main pendant complete the decoration of this ornate object which was obviously made to match the crown (No. 12).

14. Pair of Earrings   Gold
Old Silla (5th - 6th century A.D.)
From the North Mound of the Great Tomb at Hwangnam (Tomb No. 98), Kyŏngju, North Kyŏngsang Province
L. 4.6 cm (each)
Kyŏngju National Museum

These earrings are characterized by a great simplicity of design and by an obvious disproportion between the large rings and the tiny pendants. They may be burial offerings rather than objects of actual use, since several pairs were found in various parts of the queen's coffin.

15. Bracelet   Gold
Old Silla (5th - 6th century A.D.)
From the North Mound of the Great Tomb at Hwangnam (Tomb No. 98), Kyŏngju, North Kyŏngsang Province
D. 7.2 cm
Kyŏngju National Museum

The bracelet was found by the queen's left wrist. The thin gold sheet is rolled back along the edges and richly decorated on the outside with bent gold wire and fine granular work. Part of the granular work forms circular, leaf-shaped and rhomboid frames for gems of various colors. This extremely delicate technique originated in the Mediterranean world and reached China during the Han period (206 B.C. - 220 A.D.). Judging from this rare example, Korean goldsmiths were able to master all the secrets of this very difficult craft.

16 a-b. Two Mounted Cups   (See Colorplate III)   Gold
Old Silla (5th - 6th century A.D.)
From the North Mound of the Great Tomb at Hwangnam (Tomb No. 98), Kyŏngju, North Kyŏngsang Province
H. 6 cm and 10 cm (left and right)
Kyŏngju National Museum

Mounted cups with openwork feet are well exemplified in Silla ceramics, but gold specimens of the type are extremely rare. Since both were at one point equipped with the kind of leaf-shaped spangles that are still attached to the taller cup, they may have been made specifically as tomb furniture. If, on the contrary, they served as cups during the queen's lifetime, one must assume that the spangles were added at the time of burial.

17 a-b. Two Mounted Cups   Silver
Old Silla (5th - 6th century A.D.)
From the North Mound of the Great Tomb at Hwangnam (Tomb No. 98), Kyŏngju, North Kyŏngsang Province
H. 9.7 cm and 9.5 cm (left and right)
Kyŏngju National Museum

These cups are closely related to the gold ones described previously (No. 16). They, too, have their rings pierced for the attachment of spangles, although these no longer exist.

Judging from the remnants of food that were found in some of these cups, they were used for solids as well as liquids.

18. Bowl   Silver
Old Silla (5th - 6th century A.D.)
From the North Mound of the Great Tomb at Hwangnam (Tomb No. 98), Kyŏngju, North Kyŏngsang Province
H. 3.5 cm
Kyŏngju National Museum

Framed by rows of petals, the main zone of decoration consists of a frieze of wild animals—mainly deer and birds—on the run or in flight. Each animal is inscribed in one of the meshes of a gigantic net. The base is decorated with a stylized bird in a circle, surrounded by a row of lotus petals. All these motifs are done in repoussé with chased details.

Thematically, as well as technically, this rare bowl reveals a strong Sassanian influence.

19. Crown with Pendants   Gold and jade
Old Silla (5th - 6th century A.D.)
From the Heavenly Horse Tomb, Kyŏngju, North Kyŏngsang Province
H. (Crown) 32 cm; L. (Pendants) 25.5 cm (each)
Kyŏngju National Museum

This is the largest of all the five royal gold crowns so far discovered in Korea, or more specifically, in the Kyŏngju area. It is also one of two crowns whose tree-shaped uprights carry four instead of three branches. Otherwise the crown is adorned according to what seems to be a well-established manner: granular work both real and simulated, gold sheet spangles and comma-shaped pieces of jade (see No. 12).

Ch'ŏnma-ch'ong or Heavenly Horse Tomb was named after a painting of a flying horse found among the funerary offerings. The only one of its kind discovered so far in the Far East, the object on which the painting appears is a mud-guard made of multi-ply birch bark.

Excavated in 1973, the tomb, a 12.7 meter high tumulus, was subsequently restored and made into a museum.

20. Cap   (See Colorplate VII)   Gold
Old Silla (5th - 6th century A.D.)
From the Heavenly Horse Tomb, Kyŏngju, North Kyŏngsang Province
H. 16 cm
Kyŏngju National Museum

Oval in section and roughly conical in profile, this gold cap was made for a king or a queen. Similar head pieces were also made of gilt bronze, silver or birch bark and cloth for people of lesser rank.

The shorter, slightly concave side is the front and the longer sloping side the back. The cap consists of several sections that were linked together by pieces of wire and tied to some kind of backing made of perishable material.

Decorated in openwork and simulated granular work, each section bears a different design: fish scales at the top, scrolls of abstracted animal shapes in the middle (compare with saddle fitting No. 52), and two different kinds of lattice work at the bottom.

Cloth caps of similar shape were widely in use in China and Japan as well as in Korea, but those made of gold and birch bark were apparently exclusive to Korea.

21. Horn-Shaped Cap Ornament   Gold
Old Silla (5th - 6th century A.D.)
From the Heavenly Horse Tomb, Kyŏngju, North Kyŏngsang Province
H. 45 cm
Kyongju National Museum

The tongue-like projection of this monumental headpiece was designed to fit in a socket located in the front of a triangular cap. Except for this projection, the entire ornament—both lateral wings as well as the reinforced central plaque—is decorated in openwork and simulated granular work with a design reminiscent of that of the middle section of the preceding cap (see No. 20). These nondescript scrolls were derived from such abstracted animal shapes as adorn the gilt bronze saddle fitting (see No. 52). In addition, again with the exception of the tongue-like projection, the whole front of the piece bears innumerable spangles which keep fluttering and glittering.

Bull horns were regarded as symbols of power and bravery by the people of ancient Silla, and twenty-odd pairs of real bull horns were found in the Heavenly Horse Tomb.

22. Horn or Bird-Shaped Ornament   Gold
Old Silla (5th - 6th century A.D.)
From the Heavenly Horse Tomb, Kyŏngju, North Kyŏngsang Province
H. 23 cm
Kyŏngju National Museum

Offhand this object looks like a smaller, stouter and more compressed variant of the preceding one (No. 21). Here, however, what was a very modest median projection has grown into a conspicuous heart-shaped horn, and the intricate openwork scrolls have been replaced by a few crescent-shaped perforations.

Some authors believe that this also was a cap ornament; others suggest that it might have been a headpiece for a horse. Future archaeological discoveries will, perhaps, determine the actual nature and function of this impressive, but puzzling object.

23. Girdle with Pendants   (See Colorplate III)   Gold
Old Silla (5th - 6th century A.D.)
From the Heavenly Horse Tomb, Kyŏngju, North Kyŏngsang Province
L. (Girdle) 125 cm; (Longest Pendant) 73.5 cm
Kyŏngju National Museum

A slightly wider version of the North Hwangnam-taech'ong girdle (see No. 13), this one consists of forty-four links and heart-shaped rings instead of twenty-eight. The number of pendants, thirteen, is the same, and several of the pendants are common to both girdles: the realistic and stylized fish, tweezers, the tablet-like blades, the comma-shaped jades, and sheathed knives and, of course, the main pendant. However, the order of the pendants varies considerably from one girdle to the other, and this one displays in third position from the right an openwork "medicine" box which is absent in the other girdle.

Such gold belts, which were originally attached to a leather or cloth backing by means of small rivets, have no real counterparts elsewhere in Asia, although Six Dynasties' tombs in China have yielded fragments of what might have been comparable belts in gilt bronze.

24. Crown with Pendants   (See Cover) Gold and glass
Old Silla (5th - 6th century A.D.)
From the Gold Bell Tomb, Kyŏngju, North Kyŏngsang Province
H. (Crown) 27 cm; (Longest Pendant) 20 cm
National Museum of Korea

Found in 1924 in what is known as the Gold Bell Tomb (Kumnyŏng-ch'ong), this crown is about the same size as that of the North Hwangnam-taech'ong (No. 12). But like the much larger crown of the Heavenly Horse tomb (see No.19), this one has tree-shaped uprights with four branches. In addition, the two long pendants are adorned with unusual hollow gold balls and blue glass beads.

Various funerary objects found in association with the crown suggest that it was made for a king, not a queen.

The Gold Bell Tomb was discovered accidentally in 1921 and was excavated three years later by the Japanese archaeologist Umehara Sueji.

25. Necklace   Gold, jade, glass, traces of silver
Old Silla (5th - 6th century A.D.)
From the Gold Bell Tomb, Kyŏngju, North Kyŏngsang Province
L. 44 cm
National Museum of Korea

This necklace consists of one-hundred fifty-two blue glass beads, eighty-eight hollow spangled gold globes, six gold bars, and a green jade pendant. When it was excavated in 1924, forty-eight additional silver globes were visible.

A necklace of similar style was excavated from the Tomb of the Heavenly Horse (Ch'ŏnma-ch'ong) in 1973, and also from Tomb No. 98 (The Great Tomb of Hwangnam) in 1974.

26. Long-Handled Tripod (Chiao-tou)   Bronze
Old Silla (mid 6th century A.D.)
From the Gold Crown Tomb, Kyŏngju, North Kyŏngsang Province
H. 15.9 cm
National Museum of Korea

This spherical vessel for warming wine or medicine stands on three legs with horse hooves. It is equipped with a long elbowed handle, a small lid and a spout in the shape of a fabulous animal's head in the round. Dragon heads in high relief decorate both ends of the handle, one biting the circular flange that projects from the body and the other holding a free-sculpted, palmette-like ornament. Delicate floral designs are incised on the surface of the handle, and eight lotus petals stand out in fairly high relief on top of the hinged lid. The square socket located in the center of the lid was designed for the insertion of a knob, probably of wood.

Differing in style from the *chiao-tou* found in other Old Silla tombs, this vessel was either imported from Six Dynasties China or closely modeled after Chinese prototypes of the period.

27. Pair of Pendants for a Crown   Gold, jade and glass
Old Silla (5th century A.D.)
From a tomb in the Hwangnam area, Kyŏngju (Vicinity of Mich'u Wang's Tomb, Area C, Tomb No. 4, Grave No. 2), North Kyŏngsang Province
L. 15.5 cm (each)
Kyŏngju National Museum

Each pendant consists of short and long chains of hollow globes and spangles ending in comma-shaped jewels. One of the smaller jewels is made of glass and all the others of jade.

These pendants, which may have been part of a crown made of perishable material, were found in 1973 in a small unidentified tomb located in the vicinity of King Mich'u's tomb.

Excavation of this latter tomb was undertaken by Yeungnam University of Taegu as part of the refurbishing of the exterior of King Mich'u's tomb. The relationship of the group of small tombs, of which this is one, to the large tomb of King Mich'u is unclear.

28. Pair of Earrings   Gold and gilt bronze
Old Silla (5th - 6th century A.D.)
From a tomb in the Hwangnam area, Kyŏngju (Vicinity of Mich'u Wang's Tomb, Area C, Tomb No. 4, Grave No. 2), North Kyŏngsang Province
L. 8 cm (each)
Kyŏngju National Museum

Old Silla goldsmiths created many different kinds of ear-

rings (see Nos. 14, 29, 30, 31 and 32). The present ones are typical of a group which consists of a large hollow earpiece, a smaller solid ring, a median part which in this case takes the form of a small globe with two connecting loops, and finally a leaf-shaped pendant with a circular, concave projection. The globes, which are the most ornate parts of these earrings, display granular work and small protruding sockets for the insertion of gems or glass.

The earpieces are made of gilt bronze, which may be an indication that the owner was not very prosperous.

29-30. Two Pairs of Earrings   Gold
Old Silla (5th - 6th century A.D.)
No. 29 is from Hwango-ri, Kyŏngju, North Kyŏngsang Province; No. 30 is from an unidentified tomb in the Silla area
L. 9 cm (each)
National Museum of Korea (No. 29); Hoam Art Museum (No. 30)

These unusually handsome pieces exemplify another type of Old Silla earrings. The slit, hollow main rings are quite similar to those of No. 14 and the smaller ring is linked directly to a pendant consisting of a hollow globe made of wires and a finial in the shape of an inverted baluster. The pendants themselves are largely hidden under two tiers of spangles. Pendants and spangles display fine granular work, a technique which is also applied to the rings of the more elaborate pair.

31 a-f. Six Pairs of Earrings   Gold
Old Silla (5th - 6th century A.D.)
From tombs in the Kyŏngju area, North Kyŏngsang Province
L. 2.5 cm - 6.1 cm
National Museum of Korea

These earrings differ from all those we have seen so far (Nos. 14, 28, 29, and 30) in the size of their attachment rings. They form a third main group known as the "small ring" type. While they can vary considerably in shape, structure and décor, such earrings are usually devoid of spangles. They were for the most part found in relatively small tombs and probably belonged to aristocrats of lesser standing.

32 a-d. Four Pairs of Earrings   Gold
Old Silla (5th - 6th century A.D.)
From tombs in the Kyŏngju area, North Kyŏngsang Province
L. 5-10 cm
National Museum of Korea

These are additional examples of the so-called "thin ring" type earrings from the Kyŏngju area (see also No. 31). One pair has gold leaf-shaped attachments suspended from twin globe median pieces. The second has three pendants, two of which are attached to the ring by chains. The third has attachments in the shape of leaf-shaped spangles, and the fourth a bullet-shaped attachment below a hollow, granulated globe with protruding frames originally inset with stones (see also Nos. 29 and 30).

33 a-d. Four Comma-Shaped Pendants   Jade, gold, glass
Old Silla (5th century A.D.)
From tombs in the Kyŏngju area, North Kyŏngsang Province
L. 2.7-5 cm
National Museum of Korea

Comma-shaped jades (technically of jadeite) have frequently been found in tombs both in Silla and Japan, and both countries claim priority for the invention of the ornament. Examples from the Hosogoe site, Aomori City, Japan, date to the Late Jōmon period (1,000-300 B.C.), and those from the Songong-ni site near Kongju, discovered in 1974, to the middle of the 1st millenium B.C. The jades may be stone versions of animal fangs or nails. In Silla they were used widely as pendants for crowns, necklaces and earrings.

The twin pieces joined together with twisted gold wire are exceptional examples in their conception and beauty, and display the Silla genius for metalwork. The caps are adorned with granulated frames set with blue glass.

34 a-g. Seven Comma-Shaped Pendants (See Colorplate VI)   Jade and gold
Old Silla (5th - 6th century A.D.)
From tombs in the Kyŏngju area, North Kyŏngsang Province
L. 2.9-6.7 cm
National Museum of Korea

One of the two larger jades has a gold fitting with a row of tiny spangles. The other large jade and one of the smaller pieces are grooved at one end. Such grooved jades generally are thought to be older than the plain ones.

35 a-i. Nine Comma-Shaped Pendants   Jade
Old Silla (5th - 6th century A.D.)
From tombs in the Kyŏngju area, North Kyŏngsang Province
L. 2.4-6.4 cm
National Museum of Korea

Some of these comma-shaped jades are grooved (see No. 30). The two pieces with relatively straight middle sections depart from the usually curved type. This deviation may be due to the original shape of the raw material.

36. Comma-Shaped Pendant   Glass
Old Silla (5th century A.D.)
From the Bronze Covered Bowl Tomb, Nosŏ-ri, Kyŏngju, North Kyŏngsang Province
L. 7 cm
National Museum of Korea

With its flat inner side, this glass pendant has a rather archaic form, although it was discovered in the Ho-u (Bronze Covered Bowl) Tomb which is attributed to the early 5th century A.D. Excavated in Kyŏngju in 1946 by archaeologists from the National Museum of Korea, the tomb is so named because a Ho-u, or bronze vessel, was among the grave furnishings. According to the inscription on the vessel, the bronze was made in 415 A.D. in commemoration of the late King Kwanggaeto of Koguryŏ. While the green glass of this pendant probably was a local Silla product, it has been theorized that the bronze vessel was cast in Koguryŏ and sent to Silla, thus proving active contacts and interchange between the two Korean states.

In addition to this ornament, a number of pieces of jewelry, horse trappings and weapons were found in the tomb, including a crown and a gold belt, a gold bracelet and earrings, and a necklace with jade. This comma-shaped pendant was not the only glass: a lacquered wooden mask, thought to be a funeral mask, had blue glass eyes set in gold.

37 a-b. Pair of Bracelets   Gold
Old Silla (5th - 6th century A.D.)
From a tomb at Nosŏ-dong, Kyŏngju, North Kyŏngsang Province
D. 8 cm (each)
National Museum of Korea

Four dragons appear in low relief on each side of these bracelets, considered the finest and most elaborate of their type. The row of crenelations on the outer edge is reminiscent of the serrated backs of scallop-shell bracelets of the Stone Age.

38. Necklace   Gold and glass
Old Silla (5th - 6th century A.D.)
From a tomb at Nosŏ-dong, Kyŏngju, North Kyŏngsang Province
L. 30 cm
National Museum of Korea

This unusual necklace consists of seventy-seven openwork spheres made of small wire rings soldered together. The spheres are granulated, as are the contours of the five leaf-shaped spangles that are attached to each one of them. These three hundred-sixty spangles are similar to those used in earrings of the same period. The comma-shaped pendant is made of light blue glass.

39. Jar with Figurines   Gray stoneware
Old Silla (5th - 6th century A.D.)
From the area of the Tomb of King Mich'u, Kyŏngju, North Kyŏngsang Province
H. 34.2 cm
Kyŏngju National Museum

Found in fragmentary condition, this unusual jar is decorated with incised circles and vertical parallel lines and with applied clay figurines, including a musician playing a lute-like instrument, a couple engaged in sexual intercourse, snakes, tortoises and toads. The religious significance of such motifs is still unclear.

40. Jar   Ash-glazed gray stoneware
Old Silla (5th - 6th century A.D.)
From Nungch'on-myŏn, Ŭlchu-gun, South Kyŏngsang Province
H. 48.8 cm
Dongah University Museum

The basic contours and ornamental schemes of this jar are comparable to those of the preceding one. The main differences here are the high, cylindrical, perforated foot, and incised herringbone designs on the shoulder, in addition to rows of circles and striations and a row of nondescript, abstract patterns incised high on the belly.
  Jars of this type sometimes bear incised figures of men, horses and tortoises. Typical, too, of many Old Silla wares, the jar was fired to stoneware hardness, burning a dark grayish or even brownish color where not covered by streaks, splotches or an uneven coating of natural ash glaze (see No. 64).

41. Stand for Jar   Ash-glazed gray stoneware
Old Silla (5th - 6th century A.D.)
H. 36.7 cm
Dongah University Museum

The high base of this stand has two rows of rectangular holes and supports a hemispherical bowl. The surface of the bowl is divided by raised parallel lines into four horizontal bands covered with semi-circular patterns. A number of similar, richly decorated stands have been discovered in the ancient tombs of Silla. This one might have been used as a vessel as well as a stand because it has a deeper bowl than other such stands.

42. Stand for Jar   Ash-glazed gray stoneware
Old Silla (5th - 6th century A.D.)
From Haman, South Kyŏngsang Province
H. 58 cm
National Museum of Korea

This relatively large stand looks like a stem cup turned upside down. Four rows of triangular perforations enliven the bowl-shaped base, while the stem is cut with smaller triangular perforations and long, loophole-like openings. Each row of triangular perforations is framed by horizontal lines in low relief. Many vessel stands of this type, both large and small, have been found in southern Korea.

43. Jar with Deer   Ash-glazed gray stoneware
Old Silla (5th - 6th century A.D.)
H. 16.1 cm
National Museum of Korea

The large, well-made hole in the belly of this unusual jar may have been used for the insertion of a spout in some perishable material. Or it may be an indication that the jar was exclusively a funerary object.

The two deer that stand in the round, high on the shoulder, suggest some kind of cultural relationship with the northern tribes. In the north the deer motif played a major role in shamanistic rituals, and deer horns were used to decorate coffins.

44. Dragon-Shaped Vessel   Ash-glazed gray stoneware
Old Silla (5th - 6th century A.D.)
From the vicinity of the tomb of King Mich'u, Kyŏngju, Area C, Tomb No. 3, Grave No. 2, North Kyŏngsang Province
H. 14 cm
Kyŏngju National Museum

Discovered in 1973 (see No. 27), the legless beast has the body and neck of a swan and a dragon's head with big, turned-up lips from which hangs a long protruding tongue. Spiky scales project from the animal's neck, spine and twisted tail. In addition, the lower part of the body is decorated with six three-link dangles which, with their leaf-shaped pendants, recall the spangles of so many gold ornaments of the period.

The cup-shaped mouth of the vessel is located on the animal's back, and the spear-like spout juts out from its breast. The conical stand is perforated with a series of square openings.

This and the following nine vessels (Nos. 45-51) were made as ceremonial or funerary objects to be interred with the dead. They mark the first truly sculptural trend in Korean pottery and as such herald some of the delightful creations of later periods (see for instance Nos. 117, 124, 125 and 207).

45. Vessel in Shape of Warrior on Horseback
(See Frontispiece and Colorplate VIII)
Ash-glazed gray stoneware
Old Silla (5th - 6th century A.D.)
From the Gold Bell Tomb, Kyŏngju, North Kyŏngsang Province
H. 23.5 cm
National Museum of Korea

Discovered in 1924 in the Kumnyŏng-ch'ong or Gold Bell Tomb, this much traveled and much published vessel represents a warrior in full leather-plated armor on a stocky caparisoned horse. The warrior wears a hat similar in shape to No. 20 and his saddle is of the type for which the saddle fitting of No. 52 was designed.

Liquids could be poured into the bowl-shaped cup behind the saddle and then out the tubular spout projecting from the horse's breast. The ring located under the spout is probably the first element of a now lost dangler similar to those decorating dragon-shaped vessel No. 44. In fact, these two vessels have much in common. Remarkable examples of the highest degree of sophistication and originality reached by potters of the period, they are permeated by a kind of vigorous humor which seems to be one of the basic traits of the Korean artistic approach.

46 a-b. Two Boat-Shaped Vessels
Ash-glazed gray stoneware
Old Silla (5th - 6th century A.D.)
From the Gold Bell Tomb, Kyŏngju, North Kyŏngsang Province
H. 9 cm and 9.8 cm (left and right)
National Museum of Korea

These charming vessels were also found in the Gold Bell Tomb in Kyŏngju. Shaped like boats, each is placed on a high perforated stand and is complete with miniature boatmen at the rudder. The disk-shaped ornaments attached to the bows and sterns are similar to those of vessel No. 44 and imitate contemporary jewelry.

Although made as funerary vessels, they were most likely modeled on actual boats of the time. They were products of a society whose economy relied heavily on the sea for food and which, in ensuing generations, would become a strong seafaring commercial power.

47. Boat-Shaped Vessel   Ash-glazed gray stoneware
Old Silla (5th - 6th century A.D.)
H. 8.8 cm
Hoam Art Museum

This vessel is similar to Nos. 46 a-b, except that it lacks a stand and boatmen and has a more realistic, practical appearance. The projections on either side of the boat seem to be racks for oars. A number of similar boat-shaped vessels have been found in southern Korea. A ship built in 1976 to survey the ancient sea route between Korea and Japan was modeled on this kind of boat.

48. Cart   Ash-glazed gray stoneware
Old Silla (5th - 6th century A.D.)
From Tomb No. 25 at Kyerimro, Kyŏngju, North Kyŏngsang Province
H. 12.8 cm
Kyŏngju National Museum

The only Old Silla vehicle with moveable wheels discovered so far, this miniature cart reproduces faithfully all the main features of the type of cart in use at the time.

49 a-b. Horn-Shaped Cups with Horse Heads   Stoneware
Old Silla (5th - 6th century A.D.)
From Pokch'on-dong, Pusan, South Kyŏngsang Province
H. 12 cm and 14.5 cm (left and right)
Dongah University Museum

Similar cups have been found in great quantity in the Kaya area. Made as ceremonial or funerary objects, they evoke the boot-shaped cups or rhyta of Central Asian or Near Eastern origin.

50-51. Horse and Boar Carrying Two Horn-Shaped Cups
Ash-glazed gray stoneware
Old Silla (5th - 6th century A.D.)
H. (Horse) 23 cm; (Boar) 24.8 cm
Yo Joyon Collection

Apparently made in the same workshop as ceremonial or funerary objects, these pieces so far have no counterparts in Korea. They were probably derived from such rhyton-like cups as are illustrated in the preceding plate (No. 49).

Each animal stands on a flat base atop a high conical and perforated stand. In addition to some accidental ash glaze, the surface decoration consists of incised crisscross motifs on the upper part of one of the cups, the boar's back and the saddle of the horse.

52. Saddle Fitting   Gilt bronze
Kaya (5th - 6th century A.D.)
Reportedly from a tomb at Koryŏng, North Kyŏngsang Province
W. 56.6 cm
National Museum of Korea

Remarkably well-preserved, this semi-circular piece was made to strengthen and embellish a wooden saddle (see No. 45). Derived from a contemporary Chinese pattern which can be traced all the way back to the Warring States period, the intricate openwork design is made of intertwining dragons with prominent heads and claws, as well as spiky, sinuous bodies splitting into several curvilinear excrescences, some of which are suggestive of birds' heads.

The piece is believed to have come from a tomb at Koryŏng, the capital of Tae Kaya, a small state west of Silla belonging to the Kaya federation (Kaya was a collective term for a union of several small states located to the west of Silla). Tae Kaya fell to Silla in 562 A.D. as the last of the Kaya federation.

53 a-b. Two Duck-Shaped Vessels
Ash-glazed gray stoneware

Kaya (5th - 6th century A.D.)
From Ch'angnyŏng, South Kyŏngsang Province
H. 15 cm and 15 cm (left and right)
National Museum of Korea

The birds rest on tall openwork pedestals. Their peculiar charm results from the animated postures and from a striking contrast between abstracted bodies, tails and wings and realistic heads. A number of similar duck-shaped vessels have been found in 5th and 6th century tombs east of the Naktong River in North and South Kyŏngsang Provinces.

54 a-b. Two Chariot-Shaped Vessels
Ash-glazed gray stoneware

Kaya (5th - 6th century A.D.)
Reportedly from Ch'angnyŏng, South Kyŏngsang Province
H. 16.2 and 16 cm (left and right)
National Museum of Korea

Each of these chariot-shaped vessels consists of two cups on an axle connecting two wheels. The entire construction rests on a high cylindrical openwork base. In other examples of this type, the spokes of the wheels are carved in relief, but here the wheels themselves are pierced to give a three-dimensional appearance to the spokes.

Clay coils simulating ropes bind the two cups together, and each cup has a thin band around the neck, breaking the monotony of the form. Traces of a natural glaze appear here and there, and the olive green glaze is especially thick on the bases. As in the case of the duck-shaped vessels (No. 53), the exact function of these vessels is unknown. While their provenance cannot be determined accurately, it is also believed to be the area east of the Naktong River.

55 a-b. Two Ornaments for King's Crown
(See Colorplate IX)   Gold

Paekche (early 6th century A.D.)
From the Tomb of King Munyŏng, Songsan-ni, Kongju, South Ch'ungch'ŏng Province
H. 23.5 and 30.3 cm
Kongju National Museum

Together with the objects of the next seven entries, these elaborate gold ornaments were discovered in 1971 at Kongju in the intact tomb of King Munyŏng of Paekche (reigned 501-523 A.D.). The king was buried wearing an embroidered silk cap, which has since disintegrated. These ornaments, however, originally attached to the front and back of the cap, have survived. Made of very thin cut-gold sheets and adorned with numerous spangles, they represent an abstracted floral pattern with flaming projections.

King Munyŏng, the twenty-fifth king of Paekche, was noted for his valuable public works. He established a close relationship with the Liang Dynasty of China (502-557 A.D.), and is mentioned in the *Liang-shu (History of the Liang Dynasty)*.

56. King's Hairpin   (See Colorplate X)   Gold

Paekche (early 6th century A.D.)
From the Tomb of King Munyŏng, Songsan-ni, Kongju, South Ch'ungch'ŏng Province
L. 18.4 cm
Kongju National Museum

This hairpin has been compared to a ginkgo leaf or a swallow in flight. It is decorated with floral and vine patterns in repoussé and has a trifurcated "tail."

King Munyŏng and his queen were laid to rest in coffins set on a raised platform in the tomb. This hairpin was found by excavators near the body of the king, lying on a huge bronze mirror. The tomb and the grave goods found in it illustrate the belief that the deceased did not need a great supply of weapons and everyday utensils to survive in the afterworld, as the Silla believed, but instead that certain luxurious burial accoutrements were more appropriate. This custom seems close to Chinese beliefs of the times.

57. Pair of King's Earrings (See Colorplate X)   Gold

Paekche (early 6th century A.D.)
From the Tomb of King Munyŏng, Songsan-ni, Kongju, South Ch'ungch'ŏng Province
L. 8.3 cm (each)
Kongju National Museum

The tomb of King Munyŏng also yielded this set of gold earrings, originally worn by the king himself. They are similar, in their design and craftsmanship, to earrings found in Silla territory (compare Nos. 28, 31 and 32), and consist of two pendants attached to a solid ring. The pendants are in turn composed of multiple parts: one with a medial ornament connecting two plain leaf-shaped ornaments; the other with a chain of openwork globes and spangles attached to a comma-shaped jade. Both earrings are decorated with granular and filigree work of the finest quality.

58 a-b. Pair of Queen's Bracelets (See Colorplate X)   Silver

Paekche (early 6th century A.D.)
From the Tomb of King Munyŏng, Songsan-ni, Kongju, South Ch'ungch'ŏng Province
D. 8 cm (each)
Kongju National Museum

Decorated with dragons in relief, this pair of silver bracelets was worn by King Munyŏng's queen on her left wrist. Incised inscriptions on the flat inner sides give the date of their manufacture (corresponding to 520 A.D.), the name of the craftsman, and their weight, which is 167.7 and 166.4 grams respectively.

The queen died in 526, three years after her husband. She was then in her thirties, according to dental evidence, whereas King Munyŏng was 61 at the time of this death.

59 a-c. Three Comma-Shaped Jades   Jade and gold

Paekche (early 6th century A.D.)
From the Tomb of King Munyŏng, Songsan-ni, Kongju, South Ch'ungch'ŏng Province
L. 2.9-3.2 cm
Kongju National Museum

These comma-shaped ornaments with gold caps are similar to those found in royal tombs of Silla (compare No. 33). As in bracelet No. 15, the spaces created by the granular work served as frames for semi-precious gems.

60. Silver Cup with Bronze Stand

Paekche (early 6th century A.D.)
From the Tomb of King Munyŏng, Songsan-ni, Kongju, South Ch'ungch'ŏng Province
H. 12.2 cm
Kongju National Museum

Discovered near the queen's wooden pillow, the silver cup and bronze stand are separate units; the ring foot of the cup fits into a circular socket at the top of the stand.

Shaped like an eight-petaled lotus, the lid of the knob is encircled by three bands of lotus petals. The highest and lowest band are incised, but the median one is made of cut-gold sheet and stands in low relief against the silver surface. The lower part of the dome-shaped lid is incised with wavy mountains, plants and flying birds, while the cup itself bears an incised décor of dragons beneath a fine scroll.

A lotus flower is engraved around the foot.

The stand is heavily encrusted but still retains part of its original decoration of animals enclosed in a border of hatched triangles and lotus petals.

Derived from Chinese *po-shan-lu* incense burners, this cup combines a traditionally Taoist shape with Taoist and Buddhist motifs of decoration. No other vessel of this type has been discovered so far.

61. Tomb Guardian
Hornblende and iron with traces of pigments

Paekche (early 6th century A.D.)
From the tomb of King Munyŏng, Songsan-ni, Kongju, South Ch'ungch'ŏng Province
H. 30.8 cm
Kongju National Museum

Discovered in the middle of the passageway leading into the tomb of King Munyŏng, this stone sculpture is the first of its kind to have been found in an anient Korean tomb. Derived from the fantastic menagerie of early medieval China (3rd-6th centuries A.D.), this bovine creature is equipped with flaming wings on its shoulders and haunches. A single iron antler projects from its forehead and its lips still show traces of the original red paint. Some art historians believe this fabulous beast might be a Korean version of a mythological animal known in China as *t'ien lu* ("heavenly deer").

62 a-b. Two Bricks for Tomb Wall   Gray stoneware

Paekche (early 6th century A.D.)
From the Tomb of King Munyŏng, Songsan-ni, Kongju, South Ch'ungch'ŏng Province
L. 33.5 cm (each)
Kongju National Museum

When joined together, these bricks form a six-petaled lotus. They belong to one of the rows of lotus-petal bricks which alternated with geometric-patterned bricks lining King Munyŏng's tomb.

Bricks of this type were used to decorate both the walls and the ceiling of the tomb, which consisted of a main burial chamber reached by a passageway entered from the south. Unlike old Silla tombs whose chambers were constructed of stone, this Paekche type was based on Chinese brick-walled chamber tombs of the Six Dynasties period (265-589 A.D.), especially of the Yangtze Valley. The lotus patterns on the bricks also resemble their Chinese models. The Korean tombs, however, display a different brick-laying method and a different degree of ceiling curvature.

63. Cup with Animal-Shaped Handle   Gray stoneware

Paekche (6th - 7th century A.D.)
From Sŏch'ŏn, South Ch'ungch'ŏng Province
H. 13 cm
Puyŏ National Museum

This cup is decorated with appliqué beads which stand out along a line in low relief against an otherwise plain body. The handle consists of a descending animal, perhaps a feline, with a long, outward curling tail. Such sculptured animals are relatively rare in Paekche ceramics.

64. Jar with Four Lug Handles
Ash-glazed gray stoneware

Paekche (6th - 7th century A.D.)
H. 33 cm
Puyŏ National Museum

With its long conical neck, wide ridged mouth-rim and relatively slim body, this jar shape is unusual for Paekche, though it has obvious parallels in Chinese ceramic jars of the Han, Three Kingdoms and Six Dynasties (206 B.C.-589

A.D.) periods. The body is broken into horizontal zones of joined half circles separated by branching, forking and interweaving concentric lines. Reminiscent of Chinese examples and of other Three Kingdoms stonewares (see No. 40ff), the vessel is partially covered with a natural ash glaze. Falling wood ash in the kiln fused with silica and other minerals in the clay to produce this type of glaze, which ranged in color from a greenish yellow to a brown.

65. Tile   Gray earthenware

Paekche (early 7th century A.D.)
From Kyuam-myŏn, Puyŏ, South Ch'ungch'ŏng Province
H. 29.8 cm
National Museum of Korea

The low relief landscape shows angular rock formations in the foreground and along the sides. The middle ground is filled with rounded peaks in units of three. The jagged lines on the bottom represent water. Trees grow along the summit of the mountains, softening the hard edges of the hills, while stylized clouds hover above the composition.

At the lower right is a man walking toward what appears to be a temple in the center. Whether the figure is Taoist or Buddhist has not been ascertained. This enchanted landscape is reminiscent of conventional depictions of Mt. P'eng-lai, the isle of bliss in Chinese Taoist mythology, and suggests the level of development of contemporary landscape painting in Paekche.

Along with Nos. 66 and 67, this piece was among eight tiles discovered in 1937 at the ruins of a temple in Puyŏ.

66. Tile   Gray earthenware

Paekche (early 7th century A.D.)
From Kyuam-myŏn, Puyŏ, South Ch'ungch'ŏng Province
H. 29.8 cm
National Museum of Korea

The terrifying, grimacing monster with outstretched claws leaps forth from a stylized landscape, similar in feature to that of the preceding example (No. 65).

Among the works of the Three Kingdoms so far discovered, this example ranks as the most detailed and vivid representation of a monster. Contributing to that ferocious effect are the bared fangs, grotesquely pendulous body and bristling arm hair.

The T-shaped belt with rectangular insets and circular pendants is typical of the period.

67. Tile   Gray earthenware

Paekche (early 7th century A.D.)
From Kyuam-myŏn, Puyŏ, South Ch'ungch'ŏng Province
H. 29 cm
National Museum of Korea

The central medallion contains a strutting phoenix surrounded by a row of small beads. The uplifted wings of the phoenix conform to the circular composition and make an intricate swirling pattern. On each of the four corners is a quarter of a lotus blossom, which indicates that similar floor tiles would have been placed side-by-side to create a continuous design of phoenixes and lotus.

68 a-c. Three Roof End-Tiles   Gray stoneware

Paekche (7th century A.D.)
a. From the Mirŭk-sa, Iksan-kun, North Chŏlla Province
D. 14.5 cm
Song Sang-gyu Collection
b. From Puyŏ
D. 13.6 cm
Choi Su-chung Collection
c. From Kŭmkang-sa site
D. 16.5 cm
Chin Hongsup Collection
Ch'ungnam University Museum

From the 4th-5th centuries onward, ceramic tiles were used extensively to roof wooden structures (besides granite, wood was the most important building material in Korea). Because of the technical restrictions of covering Korean roofs, tiles appear in two forms. One is semi-circular in cross-section and is sometimes closed at one end with a decorated disc (the end-tile for the eaves). The other is flatter, only slightly concave in section, and sometimes bears a decorated rim. The flatter tiles were placed hollow side up, and the semi-circular tiles were laid down over the seams where the two flatter tiles met.

With Buddhist influence the lotus became the most popular decoration for end-tiles because it could easily be adapted to a restricted circular format. During the Paekche period, the flower appeared in a six and eight-petaled form, having emerged from the four-petaled shape of Koguryŏ. Later, in the Silla period, the elaborated petal count reached sixteen and even thirty-two.

It seems that decorated roof tiles were not used on private homes, only on temple and palace structures. The Mirŭk-sa (Maitreya Temple) was founded by the Paekche King Mu around 630 A.D. at the site of Kŭmma-myŏn in Iksan-kun. King Mu (reigned 600-641 A.D.) was married to a Silla princess Sŏnhwa, whose father King Chinp'yŏng sent artisans to work on the construction of the building. Mirŭk-sa is said to have been the largest temple in East Asia when it was built. All that remains today are the foundation stones, the banner-staff base, and six stories of a stone pagoda. This pagoda is the oldest extant in Korea and reflects architecturally a wooden prototype.

69. Standing Buddha   Gilt bronze
Koguryŏ (probably 539 A.D.)
H. 19.2 cm
From Ŭiryŏng, South Kyŏngsang Province
National Museum of Korea

Discovered in 1963, this image is relatively well-preserved except for the somewhat damaged nimbus. The figure has a fairly large *uṣṇīṣa* (the protuberance on top of the head symbolic of supreme wisdom) and the head is tilted forward slightly. The face is smiling. The heavy robe covers both shoulders, and there is little indication of a body beneath it. The robe continues down the front of the statue in V-shaped folds, and the hems at either side fall in fin-shaped points, a characteristic of Chinese Buddhist bronzes of the early 6th century. The hands are in the *abhaya* and *vara mudrās* (gestures of "fearlessness" and "charity" respectively). The cylindrical pedestal is topped by a single inverted lotus. The nimbus is incised in front with a flame pattern, another motif often seen in Chinese Buddhist statues of the 5th and 6th centuries.

The style of the figure, derived from that of the fully-developed Northern Wei style in China, suggests a date near the middle of the 6th century. On the back of the nimbus a four-column inscription of 47 characters gives the date as the cyclical year *kimi* (*chi-wei* in Chinese), the seventh year of the Yŏn-ga reign period, tentatively identified as 539 A.D. The name "Koguryŏ" is also given in the inscription.

70. Buddhist Triad   Gilt bronze
Three Kingdoms (dated 563 A.D.)
H. 17.5 cm
Kansong Museum of Fine Arts

Smiling with downcast eyes, the central figure of this triad has a prominent *uṣṇīṣa*, and his head and hands are proportionately larger than his body. A robe falls in symmetric folds in front of the waist, then flows out widely to either side in the "fish-tail" folds seen in the previous example. The hands are arranged in the *abhaya* and *vara mudrās*. Furthermore, the fourth and fifth fingers of the left hand are bent in a manner frequently seen in Paekche figures.

The two attendant Bodhisattvas wear three-sided crowns and have long heavy robes similar in general outline to that of the main figure. Their long, heavy scarves cross in front before looping over the arms. The leaf-shaped nimbus is covered with a flame pattern, while the circular halo behind the main figure's head is adorned with concentric lines and designs of lotus and vine.

The inscription on the back gives the cyclical year *kye-mi* (*kuei-wei* in Chinese), which is considered to correspond to 563 A.D. (probably Paekche). The cylindrical pedestal is decorated with an inverted lotus made of three rows of petals and edged with a beaded design.

71. Standing Buddha   Gilt bronze
Three Kingdoms (late 6th century A.D.)
Reportedly from north of Seoul
H. 9 cm
Kwak Yong-dae Collection

This short, charming statue of the Buddha stands on a circular platform in the shape of an inverted lotus flower. The hair is arranged in spiral curls in very low relief, with no sign of an *uṣṇīṣa*. The right hand is in *abhaya mudrā and* left hand in *vara mudrā*.

The simple, columnar appearance of this image, and the disappearance of the "fish-tail" pattern in the drapery suggest the influence of Chinese sculptures of the Northern Ch'i (550-577 A.D.) and Northern Chou (557-581 A.D.) Dynasties. These tendencies became more apparent in Korean sculptures of the early 7th century.

This statue reportedly was discovered after World War II.

72. Seated Buddha   Gilt bronze
Three Kingdoms (late 6th century A.D.)
H. 8.8 cm
Namgung Ryun Collection

This seated Buddha follows the style of the late Northern Wei and Eastern Wei Dynasties of China (early 6th century A.D.). The hands and the head, with its high *uṣṇīṣa,* are proportionately much larger than the body, again elements seen in Chinese Buddhist bronzes of the early 6th century. Draped over both shoulders, the robe hangs down below the crossed legs and falls in multi-layered folds over what originally would have been a throne or pedestal. This drapery pattern is typical of the late Northern Wei period and is found in both Korean and Japanese Buddhist art of the 6th and 7th centuries. The hands are folded over the lap and hold an alms bowl.

73. Seated Buddha   Soapstone (steatite)
Paekche (late 6th century A.D.)
From Kunsu-ri, Puyŏ, South Ch'ungch'ŏng Province
H. 13.4 cm
National Museum of Korea

Seated in the same posture as the previous example, this is one of the earliest Buddha images of this type from the Three Kingdoms Period. The head has a small *uṣṇīṣa,* and the round face is graced by a gentle smile. The shoulders are narrow, and the relatively heavy robe falls in thick concentric folds over the chest. The upper part of the chest is bare, exposing a small incised swastika (a symbol of the Buddha's esoteric doctrine). The hands are in the *dyhāna* (meditation) *mudrā.* Cascading in three tiers of schematic folds, the bottom of the robe almost covers the pedestal.

Largely because of its material, this statue reveals more three-dimensionality of form and a greater sense of warmth than most contemporary bronze images. However, these features generally are regarded as regional characteristics of Paekche workmanship.

Together with a gilt bronze statue of a Bodhisattva, this soapstone image was discovered in 1936 at the temple site of Kunsu-ri, Puyŏ, the last capital of the Paekche Kingdom.

74. Seated Maitreya   Gilt bronze

Old Silla (6th century A.D.)
From Andong, North Kyŏngsang Province
H. 15.4 cm
Kyŏngju National Museum

Seated in a posture of meditation, Maitreya (the Buddha of the Future) is depicted with a crown and plaited hair, which comes down to the shoulders. The projection behind the head once supported a halo. Except for a necklace and bracelets, the upper half of the body is left bare. The parallel vertical folds of the drapery on the pedestal and the some-what rigid, angular contour of the figure's posture suggest an early date among existing Maitreya statues.

This image of Maitreya is considered especially valuable because of its known provenance. Andong is situated within the territory of the ancient Silla Kingdom; therefore, it is likely that this is a Silla statue. It is believed that the area was on the early Buddhist route connecting Silla to the Koguryŏ Kingdom to the north, as it was through Andong that the Old Silla Dynasty first received Buddhism. Some very fine, important sculptures have been found in this region, which is considered to have been an active Buddhist center in the formative stage of Buddhism in Silla.

75. Seated Maitreya   Gilt bronze

Three Kingdoms (late 6th - early 7th century A.D.)
H. 28.6 cm
National Museum of Korea

There are many Korean figures of Maitreya in meditation, but this one, with its attenuated proportions and solemn expression, is in some ways unique. The overall effect is highly stylized, giving it an air of spirituality. The figure wears a crown, from which two cylindrical tresses fall to each shoulder. The face is elongated, as are the waist, arms and hands. This otherwise rather stern deity wears an intri-cate and ostentatious piece of jewelry consisting of a short necklace from which two long strands fall down to a point between the knees. Here they join under a floral medallion, and then pass down to either side of the throne and back up to the neck behind the figure. The left foot rests on a lotus bud. The octagonal lotus throne is supported by an open-work square plinth.

This abstract style was passed on to Japan, where it ap-peared in several of the meditating Maitreya figures among the famous "48 Buddhas" group now in the Tōkyō National Museum and dating to the 7th century A.D.

76. Seated Maitreya   (See also Colorplate XI) Gilt bronze

Three Kingdoms (early 7th century A.D.)
H. 90 cm
National Museum of Korea

This youthful Maitreya in meditation is one of the finest Buddhist sculptures in East Asia. The figure sits in a relaxed pose, very close to that of the preceding entry (No. 75). However, the modeling is much fuller and more naturalis-tic, revealing influence from the Buddhist sculpture of the Northern Ch'i Dynasty in China (550-577 A.D.). The figure's three-lobed crown is relatively simple, yet provides an elegant curvilinear rhythm reflected in the collar of the robe. The eyes are cast down, and the lips curve in a gentle smile. The right elbow rests on the right knee, with the fingers of the hand delicately touching the cheek. The left hand rests on the left ankle. In contrast to the austerity of the upper half of the figure, the drapery of the skirt falls in complex, asymmetric folds over the cylindrical throne. As in the case of the seated Maitreya just seen (No. 75), the left foot rests on a small lotus blossom, itself an extension of the base of the throne. A nimbus, now missing, was originally attached to the back of the statue.

This Maitreya is particularly significant because of the clear connection between it and certain Japanese Buddhist statues of the 7th century, especially the famous camphor-wood meditating Bodhisattva in the Chūguji, Nara, and another wooden Bodhisattva in the Kōryūji, Kyōto, whose crown is almost identical to that of this image.

77. Standing Avalokiteśvara   (See Colorplate XIII)
Gilt bronze
Old Silla (early 7th century A.D.)
From Samyang-tong, Sŏngbuk-ku, Seoul
H. 20.5 cm
National Museum of Korea

Found in 1967, this image has been somewhat damaged at the ankles and sides, but otherwise retains its brilliant gild-ing. The front panel of the figure's three-sided floral crown contains a crudely modeled seated figure of the Buddha Amitābha, the spiritual father of Avalokiteśvara (the Bodhisattva of Compassion). The eyes are cast down slightly, and the ridge of the nose is sharply defined. The hair hangs down in two long locks over the shoulders. A necklace with serrated edges is worn across the chest, and a scarf is draped twice across the front of the body in two U-shaped folds. The right hand, raised to the height of the chest, gestures with the thumb and first finger spread out.

Inspired by a style prevailing in Sui China, this effigy may lack in refinement and precision, but conveys a sense of in-timacy and naïveté which is distinctively Korean.

78. Standing Buddha   Gilt bronze

Old Silla (early 7th century A.D.)
From Yangp'yŏng, Kyŏnggi Province
H. 30 cm
National Museum of Korea

Discovered in 1976 at an ancient temple site in Yangp'yŏng, northeast of Seoul, this statue has been preserved almost intact, although the original pedestal is lost. The robe hangs in symmetric folds from the tall body. The style of this image and its provenance suggest that it may be an Old Silla sculpture made around 600 A.D. With its full, oblong face and columnar appearance, it resembles Chinese Bud-dhist statues of the Northern Ch'i Dynasty (550-577 A.D.).

79. Avalokiteśvara   (See Colorplate XII) Gilt bronze
Old Silla (mid 7th century A.D.)
From Sŏnsan, North Kyŏngsang Province
H. 34 cm
National Museum of Korea

This figure is identified as Avalokiteśvara, the Bodhisattva of Compassion, by the presence of a small Buddha on the front of the triangular crown (see No. 77). The tall, slender body is dressed in a robe which reaches to the feet, and adorned with a necklace and string of beads. A scarf loops around the body and over both arms.

The statue was discovered with two other figures in Sŏn-san, an area near Andong (see No. 74) and is stylistically related to another well-known Paekche gilt bronze figure of a Bodhisattva discovered at Kyuam-ni, Puyŏ, the last capital of the Paekche Kingdom. Such stylistic affinities indicate close artistic ties between the two Kingdoms.

80. Standing Bodhisattva   Granite
Old Silla (mid 7th century A.D.)
From Samhwa-ryŏng, Kyŏngju, North Kyŏngsang Province
H. 90.8 cm
Kyŏngju National Museum

This stone image was originally one of two attendant figures flanking a statue of Maitreya, the Buddha of the Future. The Bodhisattva wears a simple three-lobed crown, and the head is framed by a plain round halo. The drapery is carved very simply, primarily on the front of the statue. The head is proportionately larger than the body.

As a whole the figure follows the sculptural style of the Sui Dynasty (589-618 A.D.) of China, which would support the mid 7th century date. However, it is a good example of the use of granite in Buddhist sculpture, which is a characteristic Korean medium and a relatively difficult stone to carve. Found enshrined in a small niche on Namsan, a mountain south of Kyŏngju, this figure may be identical to the statue mentioned in an ancient record as having been carved and placed at the site in 644 A.D.

81. Two Guardian Figures (Lokāpalas) (See Colorplate XIV)   Bronze
Unified Silla (ca. 682 A.D.)
From the Site of Kamŭn-sa, North Kyŏngsang Province
H. 20.5 cm and 21.6 cm
National Museum of Korea

Discovered in 1959 in the western pagoda at the site of Kamŭn-sa some 20 miles east of Kyŏngju, these figures were originally attached to the exterior of a square bronze relic container *(śarīra)*. The temple to which the pagoda belongs is known from historic records to have been built in 682 A.D., and it is assumed that the relics are of the same date. The guardian holding a pagoda and standing on the shoulders of a dwarfish demon represents Vaiśravana, the Guardian of the North. The other, who stands on a deer and holds a lance in the left hand, may be identified from the sculpture's position at the time of discovery as Dhritarāṣtra, the Guardian of the East. They both are clothed in armor and have fierce facial expressions. Comparison with similar Chinese and Japanese figures of the same period suggests strong influence from T'ang China (618-906 A.D.). A guardian stepping on an animal instead of a demon is rare in Korea, but common in India.

82. Bhaiṣajyaguru   Gilt bronze
Unified Silla (late 7th century A.D.)
H. 29.6 cm
National Museum of Korea

The worship of Bhaiṣajyaguru, the Buddha of Medicine, originated in China during the 6th century A.D. Bronze figures of this Buddha, however, are most commonly found in Korea and Japan. He is often seen seated on a lotus throne and accompanied by the Bodhisattvas of the Sun and Moon, with whom he rules over a Paradise in the East (similar to the Western Paradise of the Buddha Amitābha). This solemn standing figure is shown holding a medicine bowl in the left hand, and is one of the best gilt bronze statues of the early Unified Silla period. Aside from the lost pedestal, it has been preserved intact. An unusual feature of the figure is that the entire right arm was cast separately.

The round, full face with its rather stern expression, the largely exposed torso and the broad shoulders are in close stylistic affinity with contemporary T'ang sculptures. The mannerism of the rippling drapery with its ribbon-like bands and its serrated edge belongs to the so-called Udayana style which ultimately harks back to early Indian prototypes of the Gandharan region.

83. Amitābha   Gold
Unified Silla (dated 706 A.D.)
From a stone pagoda at the Hwangbok-sa site, Kyŏngju, North Kyŏngsang Province
H. 12.2 cm
National Museum of Korea

Complete with pedestal and openwork nimbus, this solid gold seated image is believed from its *mudrā* and from the inscription inside the lid of the bronze box where it was found to represent Amitābha, the Buddha of the Western Paradise or Pure Land. The drapery and modeling of the figure are executed in the prevailing style of the contemporary T'ang Dynasty in China. The throne is decorated with lotus petals around the base, and the figure is backed by an openwork, flame-shaped nimbus and a lotus-shaped halo.

This is one of two solid gold statues discovered in 1942 in a gilt bronze box located in the second story of a stone pagoda at the site of Hwangbok-sa (Hwangbok Monastery) on Nangsan (Mt. Nang), on the eastern outskirts of Kyŏngju. According to the inscription written on the *śarīra* (relic) box, this image must have been the one placed in the pagoda in 706 A.D. by the Silla King Sŏngdŏk (r. 702-737).

84. Bhaiṣajyaguru   Gilt bronze
Unified Silla (8th century A.D.)
H. 37 cm
National Museum of Korea

This heavy-set standing figure of Bhaiṣajyaguru originally would have held a medicine bowl *(patrā)* in the left hand, indicating this Buddha's status as a divine healer. The figure's robes are depicted in the "rolling wave" style which originated in China during the early T'ang Dynasty (618-906 A.D.). Unlike No. 82, such massive images were quite widespread in 8th century Korea and also appear frequently in Buddhist wooden sculpture of the early Heian Period in Japan (794-897 A.D.). The solemn expression of the face is characteristic of late Silla sculpture, a feature also shared with 8th-9th centuries Tempyō and Heian images.

85. Buddha Triad   (See Colorplate XV)   Gilt bronze
Unified Silla (8th century A.D.)
From Anap-chi, Kyŏngju, North Kyŏngsang Province
H. 27 cm
Kyŏngju National Museum

A masterpiece of its kind, this triad was cast in a single piece along with the halo and throne, and is believed to have been part of a miniature wooden shrine. Seated on a lotus flower, the central Buddha is shown making the *dharmacakra mudrā* (the gesture of "turning the wheel" of the *Dharma*, or Buddhist Law), and consequently may represent Amitābha. In that case, the Bodhisattvas on either side would be Avalokiteśvara and Mahāsthāmaprapta. They are backed by an openwork nimbus with outer border of floral scrolls. The triad is cast in a T'ang Dynasty style, as exemplified by the full modeling of the figures and the *tribhaṅga* ("triple-bend") postures of the Bodhisattvas. Furthermore, the triad recalls the well-known 8th century Japanese Amida triad in repoussé belonging to the Hōryuji (now in the Tōkyō National Museum), and reflects the strong stylistic ties between the two countries during the 8th century.

The triad was excavated in 1975 with numerous other bronze and gold objects, ceramic roof tiles, and a wooden boat at the Anap-chi (Anap Pond) site in Kyŏngju, originally a small artificial lake in the Silla capital adjoining a palace of the late 7th century.

86. Seated Bodhisattva   Gilt bronze
Unified Silla (8th century A.D.)
From Anap-chi, Kyŏngju, North Kyŏngsang Province
H. 27 cm
Kyŏngju National Museum

Cast in the same openwork technique as No. 85, this image is one of several Bodhisattvas discovered at the Anap-chi site in 1975. Backed by a flaming nimbus and wearing a high crown and jewelry, the figure is seated in meditation on a lotus throne. The Bodhisattva makes an esoteric Buddhist gesture of adoration, the *añjali mudrā*, which may indicate that this is a manifestation of the Bodhisattva Mahāsthāmaprapta, and consequently an important and rare example of early Esoteric Buddhist sculpture in Silla.

The long tenons at the bottom were inserted in a base, probably that of a wooden shrine.

87. Avalokiteśvara   Gilt bronze
Unified Silla (early 8th century A.D.)
H. 18.1 cm
Cha Myong-ho Collection

With the presence of the seated Buddha Amitābha in his crown, this deity can be identified as the Bodhisattva Avalokiteśvara, several examples of which are included in the exhibition (see e.g. Nos. 77 and 79). The pedestal and halo of the figure are missing, and the face has been damaged slightly. An ornate necklace hangs from the neck. A scarf is draped over the shoulders, which are otherwise bare. The skirt-like robe is gathered at the waist with one of the floral medallions attached to the jeweled strands hanging from the necklace. Both the highly rhythmic treatment of the drapery and the figure's elegant stance reflect the height of the T'ang style prevailing in early 8th century China.

88. Bodhisattva   Gilt bronze
Unified Silla (8th century A.D.)
H. 11.65 cm
Yun Jang-sop Collection

This small but robust statue, holding a holy vase in the left hand, is possibly a representation of Avalokiteśvara. The figure stands upright in a relatively static position and is dressed very simply in a *dhoti* and scarf, without the usual heavy jewelry. The pensive expression of the face, the simplified and symmetrical drapery folds, and the high lotus pedestal placed on an openwork octagonal base are all local features which seem to have developed sometime after the middle of the 8th century.

89. Head of Vajrapani   Granite
Unified Silla (mid 8th century A.D.)
From Sŏkkuram, Kyŏngju, North Kyŏngsang Province
H. 56 cm
Kyŏngju National Museum

This head belongs to one pair of Buddhist guardian figures, originally placed on either side of the entrance to the well-known Sŏkkuram cave-temple in Kyŏngju and discovered during reconstruction work in 1913-15. The sculpture is believed to have been carved prior to those standing in the cave-temple itself. The high chignon, the fierce eyes and the grimacing features of the face are powerfully represented. The deep modeling gives the piece a divine, supernatural quality, a feature also found in the main Buddha and other reliefs in the cave.

90. Zodiac Figure of a Monkey   Granite
Unified Silla (8th century A.D.)
Reportedly from the tomb of King Sŏngdŏk, Kyŏngju, North Kyŏngsang Province
H. 104 cm
Kyŏngju National Museum

Originally brought from what is thought to be the tomb of King Sŏngdŏk (reigned 702-736 A.D.) in Kyŏngju, this figure represents a monkey and corresponds to the direction West/Southwest. His face has been damaged. He holds a sword and is dressed in a heavy robe over a suit of armor.

Many anthropomorphic figures of the twelve signs of the zodiac were sculpted during the Unified Silla period to protect buildings and tombs. With animal heads and human bodies, they appear both in the round (as in this example) and in relief on stone panels.

There are several royal tombs in Kyŏngju which are surrounded by zodiac figures. Some are dressed in armor, while others are represented in civilian clothes.

91. Pillar with Stretching Lion
   (See Colorplate XVII)   Granite
Unified Silla (8th - 9th century A.D.)

H. 99 cm
Kyŏngju National Museum

This rectangular granite pillar is carved in high relief with the back view of a lion stretching upwards with its paws. The pillar probably served as a cornerstone or as a suppor for a lost monument. The graceful contour of the lion, the sense of volume provided by the rounded surfaces, accentuated by simple, incised lines for mane and tail—all contribute to make this large-scale work a superb example of Silla sculpture.

Lions sculptured in stone were frequently used as supports for stone lanterns or other architectural monuments during the Unified Silla period, and were usually depicted crouching or standing erect on hind legs.

92. Seated Buddha   Cast iron
Unified Silla (late 8th - early 9th century A.D.)
Reportedly from Powŏn-sa, South Ch'ungch'ŏng Province
H. 150 cm
National Museum of Korea

This monumental seated Buddha is an early specimen of Buddhist sculpture in iron, a medium which became widespread in the 9th and 10th centuries. The smooth modeling of the face, the broad shoulders, simplified drapery and skillful casting technique make this one of the finest early examples of Korean cast iron Buddhas and one of the most spectacular of its kind in Far Eastern Asia. The missing hands must have been in the *bhūmisparśa mudrā* (the ''earth-touching'' gesture), like the Buddha Sŏkkuram.

This statue is said to have been moved to the National Museum from the Powŏn-sa (Powŏn Temple or Monastery) site in South Ch'ungch'ŏng Province.

93. Two Dragon Heads   Gilt bronze and copper plate
Unified Silla (7th - 8th century A.D.)
From Anap-chi, Kyŏngju, North Kyŏngsang Province
L. 15.7 cm (each)
Kyŏngju National Musueum

Each dragon head has five holes for attachment to a hard surface, and they are believed to have adorned the armrests of a chair. The tongues are made separately of copper plate inserted into the mouth.

94. Snuffers   Gilt bronze
Unified Silla (7th - 8th century A.D.)
From Anap-chi, Kyŏngju, North Kyŏngsang Province
L. 25.5 cm (each)
Kyŏngju National Museum

Presumably once gilded, these bronze snuffers were used to cut off the burnt portion of lamp wicks. They were unearthed from the Anap-chi site, which yielded many other utilitarian objects as well. The scalloped, rhythmically curving silhouettes of the handles are complemented by arabesques of leafy scrolls set against a dotted background.

A similar pair has been preserved in the Shōsoin in Nara, Japan, but they lack the arabesque patterns and wick receiver seen in this example.

95 a-d. Gold Śarīra Casket, Glass Śarīra Bottle, Four Gold
   Tablets Inscribed with Buddhist Sūtra and Gold Case
   for Sūtra Tablets
   (See also Colorplate XVI)
Unified Silla (8th century A.D.)
From the stone pagoda at Wanggung-ni, Iksan-kun, North Chŏlla Province
H. (Casket) 10.3 cm; (Bottle) 6.1 cm; (Tablets) 14.8 cm; (Tablet Case) 6.3 cm
National Museum of Korea

The sides of the gold casket for Buddhist relics (*śarīra*) are decorated with a punched design outlining flower petals, and there is a lotus-shaped knob on the lid. The slender-necked bottle of dark green glass was found on a lotus pedestal within the casket. The gold stopper of the bottle is in the shape of a lotus bud. The Buddhist text of the *Prajñāpāramitā Sūtra* (*Sūtra on the Perfection of Wisdom*) was written in repoussé on nineteen leaves of thin gold sheets in Chinese regular script (*k'ai-shu*).

These objects were discovered in the five-story stone pagoda at Wanggung-ni in December, 1965. The first story of the pagoda contained two square cavities, in which these objects were found.

96. Finial in Shape of Dragon Head
(See Colorplate XVIII)   Gilt bronze
Unified Silla (8th - 9th century A.D.)
From Yŏngju, North Kyŏngsang Province
H. 65 cm
Kyŏngju National Museum

This forceful head is a vivid illustration of the degree of technical skill and sophistication which prevailed in the best bronze foundries of the period.

The dragon's eyes have a transfixing glare, and the curving snout, mane and ridged spine leap like licking flames. The beard, whiskers and crown hair billow out in long flowing lines. The neck is incised with overlapping fish and snake-like scales. The entire surface was once gilded.

Discovered at Yŏngju in 1976 during construction work the head is a finial for a pole which probably marked the entrance to a Buddhist monastery and would have been of the same type as No. 155. Within the dragon's mouth is a large pulley wheel which apparently was used to guide the rope for raising and lowering a large banner or Buddhist emblems.

97. Roof End-Tile   Gray stoneware
Unified Silla (7th - 8th century A.D.)
D. 13.7 cm
Kyŏngju National Museum

This end-tile reflects the diverse origins and richness of decorative patterns found during the period. The motif of two confronting birds within a bead-bordered medallion which may have originated in Western Asia, became prominent in the decorative repertory of T'ang China mirrors (618 - 906 A.D.). From there the design was transmitted to Korea where it took on indigenous characteristics. In beauty of style and technical excellence, Korean tiles remain unsurpassed and rival those made in China and Japan.

98. Roof End-Tile   Gray stoneware
Unified Silla (7th - 8th century A.D.)
From Bomun-tong, Kyŏngju, North Kyŏngsang Province
H. 22.5 cm
National Museum of Korea

99. Roof End-Tile   Gray stoneware
Unified Silla (8th century A.D.)
H. 15.7 cm
Kyŏngju National Museum

100. Roof End-Tile   Glazed stoneware
Unified Silla (8th century A.D.)
From Anap-chi, Kyŏngju, North Kyŏngsang Province
H. 39 cm
Kyŏngju National Museum

Tiles with monster masks (*kwimyŏn*) were mounted on the ends of rafters and were supposed to ward off evil spirits. Though the use of architectural tiles is said to date back at least 2,000 years, this type of monster-mask end-tile apparently came into vogue during the Three Kingdoms period. By the Unified Silla, such tiles demonstrate a flair for pictorial invention and imaginative stylistic variations.

101. Tile   Gray stoneware
Unified Silla (8th century A.D.)
From Anap-chi, Kyŏngju, North Kyŏngsang Province
H. 31.4 cm
National Museum of Korea

Balanced around a central floral medallion are scrolling arabesques based on a palmette and vine motif. Three sides of the tile fitted with similar tiles to form a continuous pattern. The edge of the fourth side displays an interweaving vine enclosing two confronting deer.

Decorated tiles of the Unified Silla period have been found all around the Kyŏngju region, not only at the sites of former temples and palaces, but also in fields nearby. This paving tile was discovered at an ancient palace site in Kyŏngju. While T'ang (618 - 906 A.D.) China may have inspired such symmetrical floral medallions and animals within vines, the lacy elaboration of floral elements and the deep and precise carving are typical of Unified Silla.

102. Funeral Urn with Cover   (See Colorplate XIX)
Olive-green glazed stoneware with stamped designs
Unified Silla (8th - 9th century A.D.)
H. 39 cm
National Museum of Korea

Buddhism dictated cremation of the dead, and as the foreign faith was assimilated into Korean society from the 7th century onward, the practice led to an increased demand for burial urns. Because these stoneware containers were the perpetual repository of the deceased, they were made with extreme care, with thick walls and close-fitting covers, and were usually interred within a stone casket.

This typical example of the Unified Silla period is a version of the T'ang Chinese *wan-nien-hu* ("10,000 years or everlasting jar") form with a *stupa*-shaped knob. On the shoulder four animal mask figures in the round were used to lash a cord over the cover to the urn proper. With its stamped designs of conventionalized flowers and plants, the overall decoration suggests a profusion of jewels, thus reflecting the brilliance and bliss of Buddhist salvation and paradise.

The urn is covered with a light olive green ash glaze which is one of the earliest known examples of intentional glazing in the history of Korean ceramics.

103. Funeral Urn with Cover
Green-glazed stoneware with stamped designs
Unified Silla (8th - 9th century A.D.)
Reportedly from the Kyŏngju area
H. 16 cm
National Museum of Korea

This small but robust box-like jar is regarded as the best example in the small group of glazed funeral urns.

The stamped decoration, as in the previous example, covers the entire surface of the object. It consists of highly abstracted floral patterns conveying an almost metallic effect.

The urn was found within a granite outer box.

104. Head of a Buddha   Cast iron
Late Unified Silla or early Koryo (10th century A.D.)
H. 27.4 cm
National Museum of Korea

During the 9th and 10th centuries, iron replaced bronze in popularity for large-sized metal sculptures (see No. 92). This cast iron head of a Buddha, a fragment of a once-complete figure originally enshrined in a temple, has a contented, inward-smiling expression. Noteworthy are the exceedingly long and large earlobes (one of which is damaged) and the very elongated, straight slits of the eyes. The forehead is reduced to a narrow space due to emphasis on the pointed snail-shell curls and the large, once inlaid *urṇa*.

The head relates to Chinese examples in its overall solid fullness or plumpness and in its blank spot beneath the rounded mound of the *uṣṇīṣa*. This last feature evidently appeared in Chinese statuary from the late 8th-9th centuries on.

This piece, however, represents a departure from foreign models in its human quality and touch of sweetness, despite its meditating detachment. The high cheekbones, small mouth and horizontal eyes also suggest local ethnic traits.

105 a-b. Shrine with Buddhist Triad   Gilt bronze
Koryŏ (10th - 11th century A.D.)
H. (Shrine) 19 cm; (Triad) 10 cm
Kansong Museum of Fine Arts

This miniature shrine houses a Buddhist triad. The central Buddha with legs crossed in meditation raises one hand in the *abhaya mudra,* as do the two attendant Bodhisattvas. The Buddha sits on an inverted lotus on top of a stepped "Sumeru" throne.

Often displaying carry-overs from earlier art traditions as well as contact with the mainland, Koryŏ Buddhist sculpture has a unique flavor. This triad is cast in an archaistic style, incorporating elements from both the Three Kingdoms and the intervening Unified Silla periods. The flame-shaped nimbuses have their parallels in those behind gilt bronze statues of the 6th-7th centuries, whereas the "Sumeru" throne is a feature of late Unified Silla.

The shrine is among the few remaining gilt bronze examples designed after a wooden structure. It is from miniatures of this type that one can visualize contemporary Korean Buddhist architecture.

106. Kettle with Cover   Bronze
Koryŏ (10th - 11th century A.D.)
H. 27.6 cm
National Museum of Korea
During the Koryŏ period many bronze kettles and bottles were produced. The type of kettle seen here influenced kettles of the Kamakura (1185-1334 A.D.) and later periods in Japan. Japanese Buddhist priests used these as ewers for drinking and for washing hands. The shape also is echoed in Koryŏ ceramic forms.

107. Incense Burner   Gilt bronze
Koryŏ (11th - 12th century A.D.)
From Pong'ŏp-sa, Ansŏng District, Kyŏnggi Province
H. 82.2 cm
Kim Yun Collection

This unusually tall incense burner is constructed in three separate parts: a circular stand with a central column and three cabriole legs, the main cup-shaped body, and the lid which is perforated with holes for emitting incense smoke. Above the cover rises a finial in the form of a flaming jewel. The large size and grandiose form of the burner make it an extremely fine and rare Koryŏ piece.

An inscription on the lid in dotted lines gives the name of a monk (Wŏn'gyŏn), probably the donor, and the name of a monastery (Pong'ŏp-sa) which was an important one during the Koryŏ period. Since the burner was discovered before the great Buddha at the site of Pong'ŏp-sa in 1967, the inscription confirms the object's association with the monastery. Covered with a fine green patina, it must have been buried when the monastery was abandoned, probably sometime during a foreign invasion.

108. Miniature Pagoda   Bronze
Koryŏ (11th - 12th century A.D.)
H. 74.5 cm
National Museum of Korea

This eleven-storied pagoda of pillar-like slenderness is elevated on a high base consisting of two platforms connected by a staircase. Between the doorways on each face of the second level stand guardians of the four directions, protectors of the Buddhist realm. The four ends of each tiled roof terminate in a dragon head, the largest and most complex being on the lowest story. The elaborate roof top ornament consists of an upside-down alms bowl, an inverted lotus, nine rings or "wheels" (appropriate only for a *stupa* of the Buddha), a "water flame" or flaming pearl (see No. 107 for related motif), a "dragon vehicle," and a sacred jewel.

During the Koryŏ period, many bronze pagodas of varying sizes were presented as votive offerings to temples. However, most of the extant miniature pagodas are quite small (the largest being only 3 feet high) and lack refined workmanship. This is outstanding in being relatively large, finely crafted.

The pagoda is especially valuable because it reveals the structure of many lost Koryŏ buildings. Of particular interest in this regard are the close-set tiled roofs, complex spire, beam, column and bracket support system, balconies, railings, staircases, latticework and relief decoration.

109. Kuṇḍika   (See Colorplate XX)
Bronze inlaid with silver
Koryŏ (11th - 12th century A.D.)
Reportedly from Kaesŏng area, Kyŏnggi Province
H. 37.5 cm
National Museum of Korea

This is an exceptionally fine example of a bronze *kuṇḍika* inlaid with silver. Thin wires of silver alloy describe the cloud wisps on the neck and the peaceful autumn landscape on the body. This fall scene includes: drooping willow trees, ducks swimming among reeds, ascending geese and fishermen. Silver also is used for the openwork fittings as well as the ring foot.

The *kuṇḍika* is a long-necked, double-spouted water vessel used in Buddhist rituals. The shape originated in India, reached China during the T'ang Dynasty (618 - 906 A.D.), and from there spread to Korea and Japan. The covered spout on the side is for filling, and the long, erect spout attached to the vessel's flaring lip is for pouring or sprinkling.

Inlaid bronze was popular in China from the late Chou Dynasty on and was particularly fashionable in Korea during the Koryŏ period. Some speculate that this metal inlay technique inspired the creation of Koryŏ inlaid celadons, and several celadon-glazed counterparts of this *kuṇḍika* exist (compare No. 130) with similar inlaid designs. The popularity of inlaying in the Koryŏ period extended not only to ceramics and metalwork, but to lacquers as well, which were inlaid with tortoise shell and wire made of silver alloy.

This piece reputedly was found in the vicinity of the Koryŏ capital at Kaesŏng.

110. Covered Box   Bronze inlaid with silver
Koryŏ (11th - 12th century A.D.)
H. 9.9 cm
Hoam Art Museum

This round, covered box is another outstanding example of Koryŏ silver inlay work. The bronze body and lid are inlaid with silver as in the previous *kuṇḍika* (No. 109). Dominating the center of the lid is a circular design of two flying phoenixes enclosed by *ju-i* lappets and a larger band of flowering peonies on an undulating branch. Curving leafy scrolls wind around the sides. The fine and minutely executed design exemplifies the sophisticated workmanship and superb technical skill of Koryŏ artisans.

111-112. Lobed Vase (left) and Wine Cup with Stand (right)
Celadon-glazed porcelaneous ware with incised decoration

Koryŏ (early 12th century A.D.)
From the Tomb of King Injong, Changdo-myŏn, Changdan-
kun, Kyŏnggi Province
H. 22.8 cm and 9.2 cm (left and right)
National Museum of Korea

Both objects reflect an early and already highly advanced stage of Koryŏ celadon. Emerging above a high pleated foot, the eight-lobed body of the base is segmented like a melon, and the mouth opens like a melon flower. Developed from the lobed vase form of Sung China, the vessel represents the Koryŏ celadon type at its finest, with lustrous grayish green glaze and refined, but stately shape enhanced by simple, incised or ridged decoration.

The footed wine cup assumes the fully opened form of an eight-petaled flower and rests on an inverted lotus. The stand has a broad, notched rim and an eight-lobed foot. Floral sprigs are incised on both the cup and stand. Chrysanthemums adorn the inside wall and bottom of the cup and a fine line design of fish swimming in waves appears on the bowl of the stand. The celadon is thought to be a product of the Sadang-ni kiln, Taegu-myŏn, Kangjin-kun, South Chŏlla Province.

The tomb of King Injong (reigned 1123-1146 A.D.), from which these objects came, yielded a memorial book bearing a date corresponding to 1146, the date of the king's death. The tomb, therefore, is of special importance in establishing a date for the type of celadons without inlay found at the site and elsewhere, for none of the celadon pieces from Injong's tomb was inlaid. A contemporary Chinese account, the *Kao-li t'u-ching*, written in 1123 A.D. by a Northern Sung envoy of Hui-tsung discusses Koryŏ ceramic arts, but also contains no mention of the inlay technique. Since the tomb of Mun Yu (died in 1159 A.D.) has yielded inlaid ware, the Injong tomb finds traditionally have seemed to suggest that inlaying came into real vogue around the second quarter - mid 12th century.

113 a-b. Two Dishes in Shape of Open Flowers
Celadon-glazed porcelaneous ware
Koryŏ (early 12th century A.D.)
H. 3.8 cm (each)
National Museum of Korea

These thinly potted dishes, coated with a clear green glaze, belonged to a set of five.

Similar dishes were found at Sung kiln sites in China and at the Sadang-ni kiln site in Korea. Related examples also have been excavated from the tomb of King Injong.

114. Covered Wine Pot with Lobed Body
Celadon-glazed porcelaneous ware with incised decoration
Koryŏ (early 12th century A.D.)
H. 26.2 cm
National Museum of Korea

With its superbly controlled variety of curving shapes—the artfully bending spout, the swirling handle, the swelling segmented body with bulbous neck and the rounded lid with petal-like rim—this example marks the independence of Koryŏ celadons from their somewhat more severe and dignified counterparts of the Sung Dynasty in China. The cover is incised with cloud patterns, while rose mallow and other flowers decorate the lower body.

The vessel resembles celadons unearthed from King Injong's tomb, but the celadon glaze under the fine, uniform clay is brighter and purer in color.

115. Bowl   Celadon-glazed porcelaneous ware with incised decoration
Koryŏ (late 11th - early 12th century A.D.)
H. 7.3 cm
Hoam Art Museum

While the outside of this relatively tall bowl with flaring mouth-rim is devoid of ornamentation, the interior is incised with a band of chrysanthemums and almost playfully curvaceous leaves drawn in a free-flowing style. The glaze is a glossy, light greenish jade color without crackle.

The foot-rims and bases of Koryŏ ceramics usually were glazed. However, the glaze on the bottom of this bowl was wiped away before the object was fired on refractory clay.

116. Covered Wine Pot in Shape of Bamboo Shoot
(See Colorplate XXIV)
Celadon-glazed porcelaneous ware with incised decoration
Koryŏ (early 12th century A.D.)
H. 23.5 cm
National Museum of Korea

An unmistakable product of the golden age of Koryŏ celadon, this vessel imitates the form of sprouting bamboo, with knotted stems for the handle and spout, and veined leaves for the body. Finely incised and sensitively modeled with carved and applied details, the leaves especially were manipulated to heighten the effect of overlapping bamboo with pulled-back or twisting ends rising to a center shoot. The glossy, grayish green glaze is very clear and almost without crackle.

Examples of this kind were excavated from the Sadang-ni kiln site in South Chŏlla Province.

117. Tortoise-Shaped Wine Pot   (See Colorplate XXV)
Celadon-glazed porcelaneous ware with incised decoration
Koryŏ (early 12th century A.D.)
H. 25.2 cm
National Museum of Korea

Whether real or fantastic, Koryŏ animal-shaped celadons often have a captivating vitality and keen sense of life that are unique. Poised with head raised at an angle, this beast is vividly visualized with dragon-like head, fangs and protruding tongue, horns, scales, claws and tortoise shell. Each of the hexagonal scutes is inscribed with the Chinese character *wang* ("king"). The dragonized head resembles carved stone tortoise pedestals of the early Koryŏ period. The handle is made of coils of twisted clay simulating lotus stems, and the animal rests on a lotus pedestal. The piece was molded, with carved, incised and applied ornaments. Wine would be poured through the opening in the back, cleverly recessed under a folded lotus leaf. The glaze is grayish green with little gloss and few crackles.

118. Incense Burner with Cover   (See Colorplate XXVI)
Celadon-glazed porcelaneous ware with openwork and incised decoration
Koryŏ (early 12th century A.D.)
H. 15.5 cm
National Museum of Korea

Koryŏ potters produced triumphs of complicated, involved decoration as early as the first half of the 12th century. This incense burner is an extravagant, but faultlessly proportioned, combination of parts. The cover is surmounted by an openwork spherical ball through which incense would have been emitted. Pieces of clay appliquéd around the brazier proper create a *tour de force* illusion of overlapping and projecting chrysanthemum leaves resting on a lobed pedestal with rabbit feet. The grayish green glaze is lustrous.

This piece is believed to be a product of the Sadang-ni kiln in South Chŏlla Province.

119. Pillow with Two Lions
Celadon-glazed ware with incised and underglaze iron decoration

Koryŏ (early 12th century A.D.)
H. 10 cm
Hoam Art Museum

The "ox-tongue"-shaped headrest of this pillow is supported by two addorsed lions, one male and one female. Roaring with open mouth and raised tongue, each lion is fiercely animated. Even the pupils are spotted with underglaze iron to increase the ferociously lively effect. Both lions have the curling mane, bushy tail and dog-like body with large claws typical of Buddhist lions. Each wears a bell on the chest. The headrest is incised with the veins of a leaf, and the base is engraved with lines suggesting folded or hanging cloth. The glaze is a lucid jade green color, without crackles.

This type of animal-shaped celadon was in vogue during the first half of the 12th century and was produced mainly at the Sadang-ni kiln in South Chŏlla Province.

120. Bowl
Celadon-glazed porcelaneous ware with inlaid and incised decoration
Koryŏ (mid 12th century A.D.)
H. 7.6 cm
National Museum of Korea

This celadon-glazed bowl is an excellent and early Koryŏ example of the technique of inlaying decoration, or filling in designs engraved in a clay body with white or reddish-brown clays. When glazed and fired, the brown inlays often turned black.

At first, as here, inlay was tastefully restrained and sparingly used. None of the three incised floral sprays on the exterior of this bowl are inlaid. Inlaid on the inside, however, are two cranes flying in clouds under a stylized arabesque band on the cavetto. The recessed center of the bowl is incised simply with a flower. The bluish green glaze is thick, with some crackles.

121. Maebyŏng
Celadon-glazed porcelaneous ware with incised decoration
Koryŏ (1st half, 12th century A.D.)
H. 44 cm
National Museum of Korea

The word *maebyŏng* is the Sino-Korean pronunciation of the Chinese *mei-p'ing* (vase for plum blossom). The Korean counterpart tends to have a more bulging shoulder, offsetting a small mouth-rim and flat base.

One of the largest Koryŏ celadon *maebyŏng* types remaining today, this example represents the special beauty of these monumental pieces. The high-shouldered vase is marked by graceful, soft curves from mouth to foot. Lotus sweep in complementing arcs over the body, the stalks outlined with strong, energetic lines, and the blossoms and leaves radiating with thinner incised lines. A squared-spiral pattern is engraved near the foot. The grayish green glaze is transparent and even-toned.

Examples of this type of celadon were found at Sadang-ni.

122. Wine Bottle with Bamboo-Shaped Fluting
Celadon-glazed porcelaneous ware with incised decoration
Koryŏ (1st half, 12th century A.D.)
H. 33.8 cm
Hong Du-yong Collection

Elegantly dignified, yet subtly daring, the profile of this pear-shaped bottle is exceptional. Fluted with bamboo, the body seems to burst outward at the belly, tapering to a slender neck which is topped by a trumpet-shaped mouth. The crisp contours and incised lines of the bundled bamboo are accented by a clear bluish green glaze which deepened in hue in the recessed and incised areas.

123. Bowl
Celadon-glazed porcelaneous ware with carved and incised decoration
Koryŏ (1st half, 12th century A.D.)
H. 5.7 cm
National Museum of Korea

The bowl is shaped like a six-lobed flower with vertically grooved sides. A spray of peony, symbol of wealth and nobility, fills the interior with an easy, swirling movement. The bowl is coated with a thick grayish blue "kingfisher-colored" glaze which has a light greenish tint.

Similar fragments were discovered at kiln sites in Sadang-ni.

124. Duck-Shaped Water-Dropper
Celadon-glazed porcelaneous ware with incised and underglaze iron decoration
Koryŏ (1st half, 12th century A.D.)
H. 8.3 cm
Kansong Museum of Fine Arts

This celadon-glazed duck holding twisted lotus stems in its bill is one of the finest Koryŏ celadons in existence. The bluish green glaze is flawless and of a type often likened to a kingfisher's plumage and described as "kingfisher-colored." A water-dropper and a fine piece of ceramic sculpture, the duck is imbued with the personality and appearance of a familiar sight, from incised feathers to head. The eyes are marked with iron pigment. On the duck's back is a lotus flower and bud. Water would have been admitted through a hole in the lotus and poured out a hole in the lotus stem on the right side of the bill. The motif of a bird holding a plant in its bill can be traced back to the Chinese T'ang Dynasty.

The duck is believed to be a product of the Sadang-ni kiln.

125. Water-Dropper in Shape of Monkey Holding a Baby
Celadon-glazed porcelaneous ware with underglaze iron decoration
Koryŏ (1st half, 12th century A.D.)
H. 10 cm
Kansong Museum of Fine Arts

Among Koryŏ ceramic vessels molded in human, animal and plant form, some are believed to be toys, while others definitely were intended as water-droppers for diluting ink for writing and painting. The function of a number of forms modeled in the round, however, still is unclear. Generally, these miniature types have survived in smaller quantity than other celadons. Often greater care and meticulous finishing was lavished on them, too.

Holes on the heads of the monkey and baby prove that this object was designed as a water-dropper. A rather endearingly intimate quality is present in the pose of the mother grasping her young and the baby reaching for its mother's cheek. Facial details are emphasized by spots of underglaze iron under a "kingfisher-colored" glaze.

126. Bowl
Celadon-glazed porcelaneous ware with incised and inlaid decoration
Koryŏ (12th century A.D.)
H. 6.2 cm
National Museum of Korea

This bowl with a slightly higher than usual foot is (like No. 120) a good example of the early limited use of inlaying on celadons. Only white clays were inlaid in a narrow band inside the mouth-rim, and the rest of the interior design is made of carved and incised floral patterns, their leaves and petals weaving in soft, pliable, swaying rhythms. The exterior is plain.

127. Roof End-Tile
Celadon-glazed ware with molded decoration
Koryŏ (early 12th century A.D.)
From kiln site in Tangjŏn-ni, Kangjin, South Chŏlla Province
D. 8.5 cm
National Museum of Korea

128 a-b. Two Roof End-Tiles
Celadon-glazed ware with molded decoration
Koryŏ (early 12th century A.D.)
From kiln site in Tangjŏn-ni, Kangjin, South Chŏlla Province
L. 20.2 cm (each)
National Museum of Korea

An inkling of the sumptuous, courtly, aristocratic world of the mid Koryŏ period may be gleaned from the high quality celadon tiles which were manufactured not only to decorate the roofs, but also the walls and floors of buildings.

No. 127, a circular ornament for a row of convex tiles, is crisply molded with a peony branch within a double circle, a ring of dots, and another double circle. The edge is curved in high relief. The grayish green glaze is relatively thick.

No. 128 a-b, finishing elements for rows of concave roof tiles, consists of long, half-cylindrical tiles with flat sides. The major decorative motifs running the length of each are scrolling leafy tendrils surrounded by incised lines.

These tiles were discovered in 1964 at a Koryŏ kiln site in Kangjin, and are among the many celadon roof and floor tiles which the excavation team of the National Museum of Korea unearthed at the site. No. 128 was the first flat roof tile discovered intact there, though the finds included many fragmentary flat tiles.

Similar architectural tiles have been located in the ruins of a Koryŏ palace in Kaesŏng and at kiln sites in Kangjin, and are also reproduced in other media (see Nos. 108 and 157). According to the official history of the time, a pavilion with celadon roof tiles was built beside an artificial lake in a palace garden during the reign of King Ŭijong (1147 - 1170 A.D.), successor to King Injong.

129. Incense Burner with Lion-Shaped Cover
Celadon-glazed porcelaneous ware with incised and underglaze iron decoration
Koryŏ (12th century A.D.)
H. 20 cm
National Museum of Korea

Reflecting the same Buddhist tradition as No. 119, the lid of this incense burner is modeled with the figure of a male lion holding a ball. Incense would travel through the animal's body and out his slightly opened mouth. A number of carved, incised and appliquéd details enliven the beast— spiraling curls and whiskers, upright, flattened tail fanning against the back, well articulated paws with sharply pointed claws, and collar with bell. The pupils are dotted black with underglaze iron. Animal masks decorate the legs of the tripod, which is incised with cloud-like patterns. The clear light blue glaze has a subdued luster.

This kind of censer is derived from Chinese ritual bronze vessels and archaistic vessels of tripod shape. There are immediate precedents in Sung and Liao ceramics. Fragments of such tripod censers have been collected at kiln sites in Sadang-ni in South Chŏlla Province. A type of Korean incense burner with lion cover was mentioned in the *Kao-li t'u-ching* by the Northern Sung Chinese envoy Hsü Ching (see Nos. 111-112).

130. Kuṇḍikā
Celadon-glazed porcelaneous ware with inlaid decoration
Koryŏ (mid 12th century A.D.)
H. 37.1 cm
Kansong Museum of Fine Arts

Under a bluish green "kingfisher-colored" glaze, the motifs on this Buddhist water sprinkler (*kuṇḍikā*) appear in white inlay: willow trees, reeds, lotus and a pair of mandarin ducks on the body, peony sprays on the neck and *ju-i* lappets on the collar. Mandarin ducks symbolize connubial bliss; peonies, wealth; and *ju-i*, luck. The tall upright spout surmounting the neck is edged with white inlay, and the lid of the short spout has been lost.

This *kuṇḍikā* resembles in shape and decoration the silver-inlaid bronze ewer (No. 109). A comparison of the two reveals the close relationship between different media.

Similar shards of inlaid celadon were found at the Sadang-ni kiln site in South Chŏlla Province.

131. Bowl
Celadon-glazed porcelaneous ware with inlaid decoration
Koryŏ (mid 12th century A.D.)
H. 8.5 cm
National Museum of Korea

One of the larger-sized Koryŏ celadon bowls, this example has a transparent glaze which is relatively thick and crackled. A combination of decorative techniques was used for the décor. Carved about the foot are double-petaled lotus flowers. The interior and exterior mouth-rims are ornamented with narrow inlaid bands of scrolls with tendrils in stylized arabesques. Evenly spaced around the inside and on the sunken bottom of the bowl are inlaid branches of lichee. Edged with a white slip background under a celadon glaze, the broad floral scroll on the exterior appears in reverse inlay beneath a zone of clouds and cranes. In this technique the background, rather than the design, was cut away, leaving the decoration in relief. The background then was filled with slip before glazing.

This type of celadon has been found at Sadang-ni·

132. Jar
Celadon-glazed porcelaneous ware with inlaid decoration
Koryŏ (mid 12th century A.D.)
H. 20.1 cm
National Museum of Korea

One of the biggest Koryŏ inlaid jars extant, this stout, wide-mouthed vessel with molded lion mask handles is believed to have been used as a container for liquids. Unusually bold in its stylized simplicity, the decoration consists of two large peony sprays in black and white inlay looming against a plain background. A clear grayish green glaze covers the body thinly and evenly.

Prototypes for such containers with animal mask handles exist in Chinese bronze vessels and in ceramic versions of these bronzes. Similar jars were found at the Sadang-ni kiln site in South Chŏlla Province.

133. Pillow
Celadon-glazed porcelaneous ware with inlaid decoration
Koryŏ (mid 12th century A.D.)
L. 23.2 cm
National Museum of Korea

Luxuriantly decorated with inlaid motifs, this pillow is said to exhibit the most refined ornamentation of any celadon pillow in existence. The headrest has concave sides narrowing toward the top. The sides have panels of peony flowers, emblematic of wealth, and the top and bottom display medallions of cranes flying in clouds (symbols of longevity). These designs were inlaid directly into the clay. Densely surrounding these motifs are thick, scrolling leaves framed by petal-like borders, all in reverse inlay.

Over the inlaid areas especially, the "kingfisher-colored" glaze sparkles with shining, silver striae like rock crystal— an effect greatly prized by Japanese connoisseurs.

134. Wine Pot
Celadon-glazed porcelaneous ware with inlaid decoration
Koryŏ (mid 12th century A.D.)
H. 29.8 cm
Yun Jang-sop Collection

This tall pear-shaped vessel has a faintly bending spout and an acutely curving handle. It once had a lid, which was fastened to the body by a string tied through the loop on the neck. The body is inlaid with four zones of decoration. Fretwork designs ring the mouth, and a band of petals the base. The neck and body are covered with an overall pattern of flying cranes amidst trailing clouds. On the body proper this pattern serves as background for medallions of chrysanthemum flowers. On the neck are clusters of circles and smaller chrysanthemums. The light grayish green glaze evenly coats the pot, except at the base where it has run down and congealed. This type of celadon has been discovered at kiln sites in Kangjin and Puan.

135. Maebyŏng
Celadon-glazed porcelaneous ware with inlaid decoration
Koryŏ (mid 12th century A.D.)
H. 42.3 cm
Kansong Museum of Fine Arts

Possibly the largest and finest example of its type, this "Thousand Cranes" *maebyŏng* is inlaid with black and white motifs which, except for collar and foot, consist of cranes flying in a setting of clouds. All cranes fly from left to right. But twenty-three of them, gliding downwards, serve as background for another forty-six which, soaring up, are enclosed in medallions and, due to this most effective *trompe l' oeil* effect, seem to stand out in relief. A collar of *ju-i* lappets symbolizing luck is located immediately below the mouth, and the foot is decorated with two rows of elongated lotus petals. A glossy grayish green glaze of even tonality covers the body.

136. Maebyŏng with Cover (See Colorplate XXVII)
Celadon-glazed porcelaneous ware with inlaid decoration
Koryŏ (mid 12th century A.D.)
H. 39 cm
National Museum of Korea

Cranes flying amidst billowing, mushroom-shaped clouds, were often used in the decoration of Koryŏ celadons as traditional symbols of longevity (see also Nos. 120, 133, 135, 138, 141 and 151). This vase, however, illustrates an unusual humanistic touch where almost caricatured birds seem to be engaged in all kinds of frolicking exercises while being set far apart under a glossy "kingfisher-colored" glaze.

This rare example of a Koryŏ *maebyŏng* with cover is believed to have been made at the Yuch'ŏn-ni kiln at Puan in North Chŏlla Province.

137. Maebyŏng
Celadon-glazed porcelaneous ware with inlaid and underglaze copper decoration
Koryŏ (mid 12th century A.D.)
H. 34.8 cm
National Museum of Korea

While this *maebyŏng* has the typical small mouth and S-shaped body, its decoration is unusual. It is one of the rare Koryo examples where underglaze copper oxide was used along with the more common inlays of light and dark clays. All inlaid motifs appear in black and white, but the petals of the large budding and blossoming peonies on the body were painted in underglaze copper and turned brown during the firing process. The rest of the flowers are inlaid,

but with such extraordinary fineness that the leaves are carefully veined, the stamens are curved and the stems and branches kept organically supple. Dainty chrysanthemums bend in arcs within valance-like lappets on the shoulder, and petals encircle the foot with inner configurations of scrolling arabesques. A keyfret pattern is inlaid near the base.

Shards of related material were found at Yuch'ŏn-ni.

138. Maebyŏng
Celadon-glazed porcelaneous ware with inlaid decoration
Koryŏ (mid 12th century A.D.)
H. 29.6 cm
National Museum of Korea

By the middle of the 12th century the inlay technique was used occasionally for pictorial, almost anecdotic scenes of this type. The bouncing, lilting rhythms of this ornamental scheme enhance delightful if sketchy interaction between people, animals and their surroundings. Inlaid on one side of the vase is a tall pine tree with randomly dotted cones and a wavy, meandering trunk. An old man, tilting his black-turbaned head backwards, sits under the tree playing a zither-like musical instrument. Nearby a crane dances.

The old man's six-stringed musical instrument is known as a *kŏmungo*. A Koguryŏ instrument popular from the Unified Silla on, it was plucked with a bamboo rod and tuned by pegs on the back and by bridges under the strings.

The other side of the *maebyŏng* is inlaid with two other cranes and a pine.

The vase has a light greenish glaze, and the base bears traces where the object was fired on silicate grit spurs.

139. Cup
Celadon-glazed porcelaneous ware with inlaid decoration
Koryŏ (mid 12th century A.D.)
H. 4.7 cm
Yun Jang-sop Collection

Children at play, or indeed human beings in general, occur rarely in the decoration of early inlaid celadons (see also No. 138). Inside the bowl three boys hold lotus flowers in their right hands and willow branches in their left and seem to be dancing around a three-leafed chrysanthemum spray located in the bottom. These motifs are inlaid in black and white while the keyfret ouside the mouth-rim is rendered only in black. The glaze is grayish green.

140. Wine Pot
Celadon-glazed porcelaneous ware with incised and inlaid decoration
Koryŏ (mid 12th century A.D.)
H. 8.6 cm
National Museum of Korea

Koryŏ potters produced many diminutive vessels such as this one. Originally a piece of string was fastened to the loops of the lid and handle. The pot presents such typical Koryŏ decorative devices as a spout incised with lines to resemble bamboo, coils of clay twisted for a stem-like handle, and floral designs inlaid in white and black clay. The flowering and budding plant which dominates the center of the body is partially reproduced on the lid.

141. Gourd-Shaped Wine Pot with Stopper
Celadon-glazed porcelaneous ware with inlaid decoration
Koryŏ (mid 12th century A.D.)
H. 34.4 cm
National Museum of Korea

The body of this gourd-shaped vessel is decorated with peonies in reverse inlay. They branch out in bold scrolls that contrast with the more finely inlaid cloud and crane design on the bulb. The neck is inlaid with lines suggesting fluting, and the glossy, grayish green glaze has no crackles.

This type of vessel originated in China during the T'ang Dynasty (618 - 906 A.D.) and persisted into the Sung (960 - 1279 A.D.). In the Korean adaptation, the constricted, "fluted" neck, the sinuously elongated proportions of the handle and of the spout, as well as the harmonious proportions of the body demonstrate the Koryŏ potter's skill in creating distinctive forms based on foreign prototypes.

142. Toilet Case with Cover, Tray and Cosmetic Boxes
Celadon-glazed porcelaneous ware with openwork and inlaid decoration
Koryŏ (mid to late 12th century A.D.)
From Yusan-ri, Changhung-kun, South Chŏlla Province
H. 12.4 cm
National Museum of Korea

This rectangular toilet case contains an upper tray and two lower compartments separated by a vertical partition. All of these elements are in openwork: hexagons simulating tortoise shell for the sides of the case and the top of the lid, *ju-i* and keyfret patterns for the bevelled sides of the lid, and floral scrolls for the vertical partition and bottom of the tray.

Originally placed in one of the lower compartments, but now located on the upper tray, is a group of five miniature containers consisting of a central round box surrounded by four crescent-shaped ones. The lids of these containers are inlaid with chrysanthemums and the sides with bands of squared spirals.

When excavated from a Koryŏ tomb in Yusan-ri in 1939, this box also contained a bronze mirror, a silver-plated needle case, and an inlaid celadon oil bottle.

143. Maebyŏng
White porcelaneous ware with celadon inlaid decoration
Koryŏ (mid 12th century A.D.)
H. 29 cm
National Museum of Korea

This vase is the earliest known Korean example of the innovative technique of inlaying white porcelain. In this process certain areas were cut out and filled with the same clay used for making celadon. When fired with an iron-rich glaze, the "inlaid" parts turned celadon.

Originally indebted to Chinese models, Korean potters adapted white porcelains, like celadons, to suit the taste of the period. Utilizing the popular *maebyŏng* form, this vase is decorated with designs similar to those found on celadons: panels of peony sprigs, reeds, willow and lotus. Stylized chrysanthemum and lotus petals, carved in slight relief and covered with celadon, encircle the shoulder and foot respectively. Typical of the rather granular-bodied Korean white porcelains which invariably have somewhat glassy glazes with bluish or grayish cast, the transparent crackled glaze has a pronounced bluish tinge.

White porcelain shards found at the Kangjin and Puan kiln sites help document the development of the ware in Korea in the 12th century.

144. Bowl   Iron-glazed marble ware
Koryŏ (mid 12th century A.D.)
H. 4.8 cm
National Museum of Korea

Different-colored clays were folded together in layers to create the striated patterns seen on this small marble ware bowl. The body was shaped on a wheel, painted around the mouth-rim with white slip and finally dipped in a celadon glaze. It is essentially this celadon glaze that distinguishes Koryŏ marble ware from Sung marble ware.

145. Cup with Stand
Porcelaneous ware with underglaze copper
Koryŏ (mid 12th century A.D.)
H. 6.8 cm
National Museum of Korea

This very thin-walled, refined and unusual cup with stand has an underglaze decoration in copper red. The copper oxide is transparent, yet splotched with reddish brown impurities. The rim of the stand is covered with such a thick layer of glaze that the underglaze red is no longer visible. Three silicate grit spurs appear on the base.

The formal antecedents for this type of integrated cup and broad-brimmed stand are found among Chinese wares of the Five Dynasties (907 - 960 A.D.) and Northern Sung Dynasty (960 - 1127 A.D.) as well as Koryŏ celadons of the 11th century.

146. Maebyŏng
Iron-glazed porcelaneous ware with underglaze iron decoration
Koryŏ (mid 12th century A.D.)
H. 27.6 cm
National Museum of Korea

The dark greenish black appearance of this *maebyŏng* was achieved by covering the body with an iron slip before applying the celadon glaze. Thus, the iron pigments impart a deep brownish-black tone, while the celadon glaze adds a greenish brown tinge. A design of white ginseng leaves is painted in slip on the gently swelling shoulder.

It is now known that iron-black wares with white slip-painted decoration were produced as early as the mid Koryŏ period. This is based on archaeological evidence provided by similar shards unearthed at the Sadang-ni kiln site in South Chŏlla Province.

147. Maebyŏng
Iron-glazed porcelaneous ware with underglaze iron-decoration
Koryŏ (12th century A.D.)
H. 27.4 cm
National Museum of Korea

Reflecting the influence of Chinese Tz'u-chou ceramics, scrolls of highly conventionalized chrysanthemums are painted with forceful directness in dark brown or black iron slip on a lighter ground. There is a calligraphic freedom and vigorous pliancy to each stroke which gives great power to the décor. The lower body is roughly brushed with a broad band of iron pigment. As in a number of other slip-painted examples, the iron glaze covering the vase oxidized slightly during firing, giving a warm sandy brown tint to the grayish-green color.

This vase tends to curve in slightly toward the waist, and so displays a typically Korean profile. The dish-like mouth also is characteristically Korean, as opposed to the flattened mouth-rim or truncated conical mouth of Chinese *mei-p'ing*.

148. Bowl with Cover
Iron-glazed porcelaneous ware with underglaze iron decoration
Koryŏ (12th century A.D.)
H. 16.2 cm
National Museum of Korea

Painted in underglaze iron, scrolling leaves with peonies are framed by bands of lotus petals on the top and sides of this covered bowl. Details of petals and veins of leaves have been indicated by incising lines through the slip, thereby enhancing the painting with finer linear textures. The covered bowl is coated with a glaze which has oxidized a brownish color. The base is low and broad, and the glaze was wiped from the bottom before the object was fired on refractory clay.

149. Gourd-Shaped Wine Pot with Bowl
(See Colorplate XXVIII)
Celadon-glazed porcelaneous ware with incised, inlaid and underglaze copper decoration
Koryŏ (late 12th century A.D.)
H. 34.2 cm
National Museum of Korea

The sleek and dramatically curving profile of this tall vessel is complemented by the broad, round companion bowl in which the object rests. The gourd-shaped body is equipped with a twisted handle and a simulated bamboo spout. The surface is inlaid with children yanking on grapevines, and clusters of grapes are further colored with underglaze copper. Similar grape decoration encircles the exterior of the bowl. The interior is incised with a large lotus leaf. The opaque and light green glaze has oxidized sporadically, producing areas of light brown color.

This is thought to be a product of Yuch'ŏn-ni

150. Wine Pot with Cover
Celadon-glazed porcelaneous ware with inlaid, slip and underglaze iron decoration
Koryŏ (12th century A.D.)
H. 33.8 cm
Dongwon Museum of Fine Arts

With softer lines than its metallic prototype, this low-footed wine pot joins a straight shoulder at an angle to a tall cylindrical neck. The elaborate, unusual cover consists of carved lotus petals leading to a winged creature perching on a lotus base. The spout and handle are modeled in the shape of bamboo, with trailing "vines" in underglaze iron. Iron pigment also stripes the neck and lotus petal border near the foot, besides accenting the scrolling branches of the lotus on the body. The white slip motifs appear under a light bluish green celadon glaze.

151. Bowl
Celadon-glazed porcelaneous ware with inlaid decoration
Koryŏ (13th century A.D.)
H. 8.4 cm
National Museum of Korea

This gently swelling bowl has a notched rim resembling a six-lobed flower. Believed to be a work of the first half of the 13th century when Koryŏ potters had just passed their technical peak in inlaid work, the bowl reflects a tendency toward elaborate, nearly overembellished decoration. An interior central medallion of phoenixes is surrounded by cloud-collar lappets and an all-over, busy décor of phoenixes flying in clouds. The exterior is smothered by bands of petals, scrolling stems of chrysanthemums, ringed circles of phoenixes in clouds, and smaller cranes in more clouds. Near the interior and exterior mouth-rims are inlaid stylized arabesque borders.

The thinly applied celadon glaze has a clear grayish blue tone, and crazing appears all over.

152. Cosmetic Box
Celadon-glazed porcelaneous ware with slip and underglaze iron and copper decoration
Koryŏ (late 12th century A.D.)
H. 2.6 cm
National Museum of Korea

The main decoration consists of six delicately stylized chrysanthemums, the pistils of which are accented by underglaze copper and the leaves by underglaze iron. Also, underglaze iron and white slip were used to create the vertical striping that runs continuously around the edges of the cover and box. Besides being a popular border device in the late 12th - 13th centuries, these stripes help serve as guides for aligning the two components together to assure a proper, snug fit.

The grayish green glaze obviously was applied unevenly, resulting in a noticeable variation in tonality.

Celadon shards painted in underglaze iron have been discovered at kiln sites in Puan and reportedly also nearby at Chŏngŭp in North Chŏlla Province.

153. Oil Bottle
Celadon-glazed porcelaneous ware with inlaid decoration
Koryŏ (13th century A.D.)
H. 4.5 cm
National Museumof Korea

This tiny bottle is thought to be a container for liquid cosmetics. Most such small bottles once had lids, but virtually none have survived.

The squatly compressed body is surmounted by a short neck and widened mouth similar to the truncated mouth of a *maebyŏng*. Inlaid decoration consists of stylized chrysanthemums within an arcade of tympaniform cells. The interstices are filled with white inlay. Overlapping lotus petals appear around the base. The glassy transparency of the glaze accounts for the clarity of the decoration.

This type of decorated bottle is typical of the wares produced at Yujŏn-ni in North Chŏlla Province.

154. Lobed Vase   Iron-glazed ware with inlaid decoration
Koryŏ (late 12th century A.D.)
H. 26.9 cm
National Museum of Korea

The rotund, lobed body of this vase rests on a high spreading foot. The tall neck terminates in a trumpet-shaped mouth, and the transition between the neck and the body proper is so abrupt that the vase almost looks as if it were made of two separate components. Such unusual profiles reflect a taste which can be traced back to at least the Three Kingdoms (Nos. 42 and 64). The decoration is in reverse inlay, and the slip-filled carving is coarse, but robust. On the body are panels of lotus flowers and leaves beneath lappets of mushroom-shaped clouds (*ju-i*). Three main tiers of decoration encircle the neck: a keyfret pattern, fungus-like clouds, and lotus petals. The foot is simply decorated with vertical, wavy lines.

Shards of similar type were found at the Sadang-ni kiln site in South Chŏlla Province and also (but in smaller quantities), at the Yujŏn-ni kiln site in North Chŏlla Province.

155. Banner Staff with Dragon Head Finial
Bronze with traces of lacquer and gold
Koryŏ (12th - 13th century A.D.)
H. 73.8 cm
Hoam Art Museum

Many Buddhist temples in Korea still have twin stone pillars at their entrances, and such pillars often supported the type of pole featured here (see also No. 96). This pole is constructed in eight cylindrical sections and is placed on a mount on a four-tiered rectangular base with a constricted waist and projecting top and bottom known as a Sumeru throne. Typically, part of the throne is decorated with lotus petals. The pole gives the illusion of being the long, lean serpentine neck of a dragon. On the last section of the pole the scales of the dragon are clearly visible, and the head seems to breathe fury through its flaring nostrils, hissing mouth and extended tongue. Whiskers flow backward, and narrow horns are set near wide-open eyes. Most of the original coating of lacquer and gold has now flaked off.

This example is believed to be a "miniature" bronze replica of the flag poles known in Korean as *Tanggan chiju*. Some temples still have such poles made of iron, but this so far is the only completely intact dragon-headed example.

156. Buddhist Temple Bell   (See Colorplate XXI)
    Bronze
    Koryŏ (12th - 14th century A.D.)
    H. 40 cm
    National Museum of Korea

A fancifully grotesque, oversized dragon with bulging eyes, big buck teeth and fangs, long tongue and snout, balances a flaming pearl in one paw and grasps a cylindrical post with the other. Vine scrolls appear between narrow beaded borders under the crown. Below and arranged in four equidistant panels are groups of nine rosette-like studs, again bounded by linear scrolls. Appropriate Buddhist symbols appear in relief on the body: large lotus flower rosettes and heavenly beings *(apsaras)*. The lower edge of the cylinder contains floral rosettes with beaded or pearl edges.

All of these are typical decorative features of Korean bells. While the Chinese prototypes may have a cylindrical post on the crown or a dragon handle for suspension, Korean bells, such as this one, often have a combination of the two. Many Chinese bells had no internal clapper, and so were struck with a wooden stick on the exterior "nipples" or studs. In this Korean example the bell was struck on the lotus medallions near the *apsaras*.

Though many temple bells were cast from the Three Kingdoms period to the Yi Dynasty, only a little over two hundred have survived today. Cast in 725 A.D., the oldest extant bell is located in Sangwŏn-sa (Sangwŏn Monastery) in the mountains of Kangwŏn Province. The largest one was cast in 771 A.D. for King Sŏngdŏk of the Unified Silla.

The classic tradition of Silla bells continued into the early Koryŏ period, but gradual changes occurred from the 12th century on. The size of the bells diminished, and the dragon-cylinder complex on the crown became increasingly larger in proportion to the body. The earlier bells had gracefully curving profiles which narrowed at the top. From the mid to late Koryŏ the shoulder line widened, giving the bells a more rigid appearance. The workmanship also became less refined, though robust.

157. Miniature Shrine   (See Colorplate XXII)
    Gilt bronze
    Koryŏ (13th - 14th century A.D.)
    H. 28 cm
    National Museum of Korea

This miniature shrine is modeled after a rectangular temple structure with sloping tiled roof. When open, the hinged doors show two guardian figures. Cast in relief on the back wall of the shrine itself is a Buddha flanked by two Bodhisattvas in poses of adoration. The triad sits in meditation on high, tiered lotus pedestals. Next to these figures appear Buddhist disciples or worthies *(arhats)*. Along with dragons on the ceiling, scrolling clouds provide a heavenly setting. On the side walls are figures of the Bodhisattva of Universal Kindness, Samantabhadra, riding an elephant, and the Bodhisattva of Transcendent Wisdom, Mañjuśri, on a lion. Originally a free-standing Buddhist image would have been placed in the interior, adding to the three-dimensional quality of the miniature shrine.

On the exterior side panels stand *lokapāla*, or guardian kings of the four cardinal points of the Buddhist universe. They include guardians of the North (Vaiśravana with a small *stūpa*); East (Dhrtarastra with a *p'i-p'a*, or stringed instrument); West (Virupaksa clasping hands); and South (Virudhaka with a sword). They are indicated by dotted lines, as are the eight ferocious guardians on the back who are in two groups above a vine scroll blossoming with lotus and other flowers. The forceful dynamic warriors contrast with the rather static figures of the interior of the shrine.

This object rests on a lotus base and plinth. Relatively small and light weight, shrines of this type were designed for personal use and could be conveniently carried. The roof has been painted, as if in imitation of celadon tiles.

158. Illustration to the Lotus Sūtra   (See Colorplate XXIII)
    Blue paper painted with gold
    Koryŏ (dated 1373 A.D.)
    H. 11.7 cm
    National Museum of Korea

This illustration precedes the text of the fifth chapter of *The Lotus Sūtra*, one of the fundamental scriptures of Mahāyāna Buddhism. In this chapter Buddha is compared to a great rain cloud whose thunder and lightning call all creatures and refresh all withered beings, offering each deliverance and rest according to his faculty. Besides the scene of figures in a temple setting to the left, the main theme of the painting is Buddha preaching to an audience of Bodhisattvas, great senior disciples and heavenly beings. Double *vajra*, or "thunderbolts," are placed around the painting and are symbolic of indestructible mystic truth. The figures, architectural settings and other details are finely painted in gold on dark blue paper.

As an act of merit and devotion expressing deep religious faith, *sūtra* copying was one of the most popular Buddhist practices. Often an illustration was added to the frontispiece of a *sūtra* to depict visually the teachings written inside. Both gold and silver pigments could be used for the text and illustrations. It is also known from historic account that the Koryŏ court had offices of Gold Letters and Silver Letters to supervise such *sūtra* copying and that the Yüan court in China asked Koryŏ to send skilled monks to copy *sūtras* and even imported special papers for that purpose.

This frontispiece resembles very closely the depiction of the same chapter of *The Lotus Sūtra* now in the Naeso-sa (Naeso Temple), North Chŏlla Province, which is dated 1415. In the Naeso-sa version, however, the style tends to be slightly looser.

159. Buddhist Vessel   Bronze
    Koryŏ (14th century A.D.)
    H. 18.8 cm
    National Museum of Korea

Buddhism reached its height of power during the Koryŏ Dynasty, and many Buddhist bronze utensils have survived from that period. These metal vessels may be extremely thin, and many foreshadow ceramic wares of the following Yi Dynasty. Nos. 159 and 160 may have been used for offerings of food at a Buddhist altar.

160. Bowl with Cover   Bronze
    Koryŏ (14th - 15th century A.D.)
    H. 17.7 cm
    National Museum of Korea

This rotund bowl stands on a wide, ridged foot. Its outward swell seems to be contained by the lid, which is shaped like an upside-down bowl. The cover angles out at the rim and slopes toward a flattened top. Rings of double circles are incised on the cover, and the entire object is marked by horizontal lines where the metal was turned on a lathe. These lines provide simple and austere accents to otherwise plain surfaces.

Such covered bowls are often found in excavations of Koryŏ sites and may have had a ceremonial purpose for use in Buddhist temples, possibly as a rice container.

Similar bowls were made during the Silla period in earthenware and bronze and continued to be made into the Yi Dynasty when the form was adapted for ceramic wares (see No. 168).

161-162. Masks of Yangban (left) and Pune (right)
    Painted wood
    Koryŏ (918 - 1392 A.D.)
    From Hahoe, AndongDistrict, North Kyŏngsang Province

Both masks here are comic and highly stylized. That of the *yangban*, or member of the gentry (No. 161) is especially dramatic with its deep carving, distorted facial expression and separately-made movable lower jaw. The word *pune* is probably a provincial word derived from *punyŏ*, meaning lady. The *pune*, a coquette, is represented with faintly smiling face (No. 162), her head at an angle as if in an insouciant, life-like gesture. Dressed as a young married woman in a mask-play, the *pune* played the role of luring the *yangban* and *sŏnbi*, or scholar. Other masked characters included a monk, servant, butcher, old lady and two lions.

These are among the eleven oldest extant masks which have been carefully preserved for centuries out of religious awe by the villagers of Hahoe in southeastern Korea. These masks were used in sacrificial rites intended to rid the local village of evil spirits, as at lunar new year. On the last day of the twelfth month (but not every year), preparations for the ceremony began. A sacred pole and altar were set up, and from the second day to the first full moon of the first month, the mask-dance plays took place. This ritual at Hahoe was held once every ten years, or at specific need. It has been discontinued since 1928.

Mask-dance plays existed in Korea during the Three Kingdoms period. Some elements were borrowed from Central Asia. The mask-dance dramas are related to the development of Japanese *gigaku* and *bugaku*. It is said that in 612 A.D. a certain naturalized Korean introduced into Japan mask-dances which were popular at the time in southern China.

In Korea a distinctively satirical type of mask-dance drama developed which was known as *t'alch'um*. These plays contained jibes at the aristocracy and monks.

Through such dramas, the lower classes could enjoy seeing members of the priviledged classes and Buddhist church criticized, mocked and ridiculed. The dramas, thus, helped provide a socially acceptable "safety valve" for the common people, as well as laughter at shared human situations.

163. Placenta Jar with Cover
Punch'ŏng stoneware with incised and stamped decoration filled with white slip
Yi (15th century A.D.)
H. 42.8 cm
Koryŏ University Museum

Many kinds of funerary jars for placenta have been discovered dating to the early Yi Dynasty. This example, unearthed from a site near Koryŏ University in Seoul, contained an inner receptacle woven of straw. The jar in turn was placed within a stone case and buried in the hills.

The body, from neck to foot, is profusely filled with bands of keyfret patterns, overlapping petals, flower heads, hatching, dense clusters of chrysanthemum heads and more petals. The lid has concentric circles filled with keyfret patterns, rolling waves and chrysanthemums.

The term *punch'ŏng* is a shortened form of *punjang haech'ŏng* (pottery decorated with a slip and a pale bluish-green glaze). Like celadon, the glaze contains iron, but the ornamentation involves a much more hasty process than Koryŏ inlay. While some motifs were incised here, entire zones were quickly stamped with designs. The gray clay body then was coated with white slip, and when the excess was wiped off, the recessed decoration remained filled with white. Fired in a reducing atmosphere, the glaze has the typical *punch'ŏng* grayish color with light bluish tinge.

164. Bowl
Punch'ŏng stoneware with incised and stamped decoration filled with white slip
Yi (15th century A.D.)

Punch'ŏng wares were produced primarily for ordinary daily use throughout central and southern Korea in the early part of the Yi Dynasty, although some of the finer pieces were made for the more discriminating upper classes and even for government offices. Many utilitarian bowls or jars were manufactured to serve or store food.

This bowl has a stately curving profile and slightly everted mouth and base. Wavy grasses appear around both sides of the mouth-rim, and a "rope curtain" of overall dots, resembling coarsely woven cloth, covers the interior and exterior walls. Enclosed by lotus petals, the inside bottom of the bowl has a central stamped floral head against a field of starry flowers. The cool, reticient color scheme of soft whites and grays is enriched by a slightly bluish glaze.

Punch'ŏng wares were particularly admired by Japanese connoisseurs and tea cultists for their sober, unaffected simplicity and rustic, free conception. The motifs taken from nature added to their appeal. Ironically, the 1592-98 invasion of Korea virtually put an end to the production of *punch'ŏng* wares, except for a few made exclusively for the Japanese tea ceremony market.

This particular kind of *punch'ŏng* ware is associated with a number of kiln sites in South Chŏlla Province, such as Muan, Yŏnggwang, Kwangju, Sunch'ŏn, Posŭng, and Hamp'yŏng.

165. Flask   (See Colorplate XXIX)
Punch'ŏng glazed stoneware with slip-covered, incised and sgraffito decoration
Yi (15th century A.D.)
H. 21.7 cm
Yun Jang-sop Collection

Punch'ŏng stonewares have been classified according to decorative style and technique. This type of *punch'ŏng* ware involves dressing the body with white slip, incising the details and scraping away the background to expose boldly simplified design elements. The abstracted forms commonly are based on such plant and animal motifs as lotus, peonies, birds and fish.

166. Wine Flask   (See Colorplate XXIX)
Punch'ŏng glazed stoneware painted with underglaze iron-oxide and ash mixture and with incised and sgraffito decoration
Yi (15th century A.D.)
H. 9.4 cm
National Museum of Korea

This flask, also known as a pilgrim's bottle, is shaped like a closed mollusk shell, or a tortoise, and exemplifies a distinctive type of *punch'ŏng* ware. After the coarse clay body was dipped in white slip and air-dried, the outlines of the peonies were drawn. The background then was cut away and painted with iron-rich clay. In the final stages before firing, the object was glazed. Because of this technique, the glaze has taken on a richer, darker blue-green tonality in the recessed areas, thus creating an interplay of dark and light hues. Pools and dripping ridges of glaze add a carefree note, as do the loosely open flowers which trail over boundaries on the top side.

This type of *punch'ŏng* ware was produced at the Kŭmgok kiln on Mt. Mudŭng, in the area around Kwangju, South Chŏlla Province. The Mt. Mudŭng potters are said to have made celadons in the late Koryŏ period, and *punch'ŏng* stonewares and white porcelains in the early Yi.

167. Bottle
Punch'ŏng glazed stoneware with iron sprayed and inlaid decoration
Yi (15th century A.D.)
H. 29.9 cm

This piece is a rare example of decoration sprayed with underglaze iron. The bottle itself has an inflated body narrowing to a neck with everted mouth. After the foot-ring was luted on, iron pigment was sprayed over the surface. Then peonies, inverted lotus petals and concentric circle borders were inlaid in white clay. Though the iron-sprayed décor is unusual, the clay and glaze are basically the same as those found in ordinary *punch'ŏng* wares.

168. Bowl with Cover   White porcelain
Yi (15th century A.D.)
H. 22.5 cm
Yun Jang-sop Collection

In contrast to the rigid formality of porcelains used at court or in official ceremonies, this covered rice bowl for everyday use exudes informal warmth and purity. Precedents for the stark simplicity of the shape exist in Koryŏ bronze vessels (see No. 160), yet this piece retains the ample volume characteristic of *punch'ŏng* wares.

169. Bowl   White porcelain with inlaid iron decoration
Yi (15th century A.D.)
H. 7.6 cm
Dongwon Museum of Fine Arts

Eloquent in its simplicity of shape and decoration, a special kind of inlaid porcelain emerged in the early Yi Dynasty out of the Koryŏ white porcelain tradition (see No. 143). This thin-walled bowl has a deep body with slanting hip, and sharply, but finely articulated mouth-rim. It is given an air of stability and sturdiness by the squared-off foot. The inlaid iron-black motifs are distilled into the briefest of contours and silhouettes drawn with ease and assurance. A band of grass is isolated around the inner mouth. On the exterior, lotus hang from long arching tendrils and rise on slender stems in half circles. A silk-sheer glaze was thinly applied, and smudges are visible near the iron inlay.

170. Bottle   White porcelain with inlaid iron decoration
Yi (early 15th century A.D.)
H. 28.8 cm
Yun Jang-sop Collection

This kind of pear-shaped bottle with short flaring neck and wide-girthed body resting on a ring-foot harks back to the celadon bottle shapes of the late Koryŏ period. The shape continued in both *punch'ŏng* and white porcelain wares of the early Yi Dynasty.

Complementing the bottle's voluminous curves is the flaring grace of the linear design: circles and wavy lines on the neck and a peony-like flower and bee motif on the body. The freehand drawing is so perfectly simplified that each line renders nothing more than the absolute essentials.

The body is made of a refined, well-levigated clay and is very thinly potted.

A kiln site which made inlaid porcelains during the early Yi Dynasty has been located at Ponch'ŏn-ni, Kwangju, Kyŏnggi Province. However, the exact kiln site that produced this bottle, or the preceding bowl, is unknown

171. Maebyŏng
White porcelain with underglaze blue decoration
Yi (dated 1489 A.D.)
H. 48.7 cm
Dongkuk University Museum

Pine and bamboo, symbols of the Confucian virtues of steadfastness, strength and flexibility, are painted in underglaze blue on this *maebyŏng*.

This vase is a variation of the *maebyŏng* form and reflects Chinese models of the 15th century in its massive scale, emphatically broad shoulder and constricted waist. The organization of pine and bamboo into a kind of overall continuous landscape scene is also typical of contemporary Ming examples, where ceramics become surfaces for painting like handscrolls. The sense of concreteness and solidity of forms in shallow, well-defined space are also inspired by Ming models.

This particular vase is important in the study of the evolution of underglaze blue decoration in Korea because it is dated. An inscription on the inside of the neck reads: Hong-ch'i, second year. This is equivalent to 1489 A.D. (Hong-ch'i is the Korean version of Hung-chih, the reign period of the Chinese Emperor Hsiao-tsung who ruled 1488-1505 A.D.).

172. Jar with Cover
White porcelain with underglaze blue decoration
Yi (15th century A.D.)
H. 29.6 cm
Yun Jang-sop Collection

The sturdy bulky shape of this jar is softened by subtle inclinations and angles. There is a slight inward slope from shoulder to base, and the proportionately small and narrow lid with lotus knob is painted with dots like a constellation. Flowering branches of wild plum curve around the stomach of the jar, framed above and below by rows of long empty petals (for more on the wild plum see No. 224). A milky white glaze covers the jar.

173. Jar with Cover   (See Colorplate XXX)
White porcelain with underglaze blue decoration
Yi (15th century A.D.)
H. 16.5 cm
National Museum of Korea

Though generally indebted to Chinese prototypes in shape and decoration, this small jar is distinctively Korean. The lid, mouth and body represent characteristic features of early Yi Dynasty blue-and-white. Typical of the period are the flaring hat-shaped lid with knob fashioned like a lotus bud; the broad tapering neck; the opulent, curving shoulder; and the pronounced inward-outward flow of the lower body and foot. The sense of spontaneous enjoyment of nature this jar conveys also contrasts with more idealized and controlled Chinese models.

The scene is filled with an irresistible rustic quality as one magpie screeches to another on a blossoming plum tree, and chrysanthemum-like flowers provide a setting. The lid is decorated with a branch of budding prunus and bamboo.

174. Water-Dropper
White porcelain with underglaze blue decoration
Yi (15th century A.D.)
H. 7.7 cm
National Museum of Korea

Water-droppers are used to pour water on an inkstone for diluting ink. They come in many different shapes and bear various decorative schemes (see Nos. 124-125, 207-208, 210, 212, 214 and 218).

This shell-shaped specimen is painted with a pine, one of the "four gracious plants" and "ten longevities" of Korean folklore. A popular motif for water-droppers, this symbol of longevity and endurance often appears, as here, by itself. The rich gradations of blue are partly due to a mixture of imported Chinese and Korean pigments.

175. Jar
White porcelain with underglaze iron decoration
Yi (16th century A.D.)
H. 40 cm
National Museum of Korea

Like a monochrome ink painting, the bamboo and plum on either side of the body appear in brownish black against a white background. Stylized waves provide a border around the base, and large lappets with jewel-like strands surround the shoulder. Coiling spirals reminiscent of conch shells are drawn around the neck.

Painting with iron pigment was a popular medium during the Yi Dynasty (see for example, Nos. 177-180). In contrast to the work of provincial potters who lacked the time or inclination to perfect their products, such monumental pieces as this reflect the greatest technical refinement. The calligraphic excellence of the brushwork suggests this may have been painted by an artist from the Painting Bureau, for bamboo demands the highest skill from a painter (see Nos. 188-189).

176. Flask
Punch'ŏng stoneware with incised and sgraffito decoration
Yi (16th century A.D.)
H. 25.6 cm
Park Jun-hyong Collection

Coated all over with slip, this flask is decorated with roundels of fish on the broad sides. The basic features of these creatures are reduced to a kind of shorthand, so there is a refreshing naiveté to their portrayal. Their open-mouth expressions and their casual off-center poses (one fin even breaks through the border) also seem like fancifully condensed images of sporting fish.

Cut through the slip on the narrow sides are panels of formalized leaves in sgraffito and a strapwork of incised interlocking geometric patterns. The asymmetrical, flattened round shape of the vessel is typical of *punch'ŏng* ware (see also No. 165).

According to some scholars, there are both chronological and geographical changes noticeable in the evolution of *punch'ŏng* wares. The earliest Yi types are relatively neatly carved, stamped and slip-filled (see Nos. 163-166), while slightly later types include more uninhibited incised and sgraffito designs (as here), loosely painted brush-marked wares (Nos. 177-178), and mixed styles (No. 179). It has also been theorized that in the early stages in South Chŏlla Province separate groups of kilns specialized in certain types of decoration while, slightly later, in kilns in south-central Korea, various styles appeared together. Kyeryong-san potters, for example, (Nos. 177-178) were highly versatile.

177. Jar
Punch'ŏng stoneware with white slip and underglaze iron decoration
Yi (16th century A.D.)
H. 10.1 cm
Dongah University Museum

Rugged in its irregularity, this jar was coarsely painted with white slip around the upper half. The application was cursory and uneven, exposing the bare darker clay beneath and leaving traces of the path of the brush which was made of the grain ends of rice straw. Spiraling arabesques exuding whirlwind energy then were painted over the slip in underglaze iron. No attempt was made to cover the lower half, where impurities in the clay are visible and where ridges are reminders of the potting process when the jar was thrown on a wheel.

Most of the *punch'ŏng* wares with similar designs in underglaze iron are believed to be products of kilns at the foot of Mt. Kyeryong. Located near Taejŏn in South Ch'ungch'ŏng Province, the hilly area is famous for its scenic beauty. The dark black appearance of the underglaze painting is said to be due to the presence in the iron of local manganese from the mountain. The Kyeryong-san kilns were listed among the 185 stoneware and 136 (or 139 by another count) porcelain kilns in the official annals of King Sejong's reign (1419 - 1450 A.D.). Yet little was known

about them until the late 1920's when investigation uncovered evidence of over ten kilns producing a wide range of *punch'ŏng* types. Inscriptions found there apparently associated some Kyeryong-san *punch'ŏng* with the "Court Protocol Office" and the "Royal Household Office."

178. Bottle
Punch'ŏng stoneware with white slip and underglaze iron decoration
Yi (16th century A.D.)
H. 18.7 cm
Yun Jang-sop Collection

Changgun is the Korean word for this shape which served as a container for liquids. There are two bases, so that the bottle could be set either horizontally or vertically. The slip covering the dark grayish clay body was trailed over the clay in sweeping motions, leaving thick puddles and dripping or splashed edges. Abstract floral designs were painted in underglaze iron around the neck and upper body, and each stroke may be appreciated for its varying pressure, momentum, and density of pigment. The body is vertically segmented by rings drawn almost with abandon around the sides.

Like No. 177, this bottle is also considered to be a product of one of the kilns in the Mt. Kyeryong area. The Kyeryong-san kiln sites were associated with Buddhist monasteries in the vicinity from the Koryŏ period on, and indeed Buddhist monks made a living manufacturing pottery there.

179. Jar
Punch'ŏng stoneware with underglaze iron and stamped decoration filled with white slip
Yi (16th century A.D.)
H. 27 cm
Hoam Art Museum

This *punch'ŏng* jar is uncommon, being decorated with both stamped patterns filled with white slip and painted designs. Two fish, one primarily stamped and the other painted in underglaze iron, swim around the body between lotus flowers. There is a quiet mystery to the fish seen here with its muted stamped designs and great striped fins.

180. Bottle
Punch'ŏng ware with white slip and underglaze iron decoration
Yi (16th century A.D.)
H. 28.6 cm
Dongwon Museum of Fine Arts

Painted with dashing strokes of the brush, the two fish on either side of this bottle seem to dart through underwater vegetation provided by stylized lotus. Even though these fish are highly stylized, they appear alert and alive with energy. The bottle is otherwise plain except for concentric circles around the body and neck and variations in texture and tone in the slip-covered surface. There are fine crackles in the glaze which has a light yellowish tinge.

Punch'ŏng wares produced at the Kyeryong-san kilns are characterized by this type of unrestrained and fluent underglaze iron decoration.

181 d. Four Landscapes
Attributed to An Kyŏn (1418 A.D. - ?)
Yi, Four album leaves, ink and light colors on silk
H. 35.8 cm (each)
National Museum of Korea

These four scenes belong to a ten-leaf album of landscapes traditionally attributed to An Kyŏn, a member of the Painting Bureau, *Tohwasŏ*) during the early Yi period. Each leaf is dominated by monumental mountains, but each also gives prominence to mountain and fishing villages, some with figures visible in open dwellings and pavilions. Of the four leaves, a and b are wintry landscapes, for they show snow-covered peaks, bare trees and overcast skies. The other two leaves do not give any clear indication of season.

Through his close association with Prince Anp'yŏng, An Kyŏn had access to the prince's superb collection of Chinese paintings and calligraphy, which included more than a dozen paintings by the Northern Sung master Kuo Hsi (active 1060-1075 A.D.). Kuo's work and that of Li Ch'eng (active second half of the 10th century A.D.) formed the basis of the Li-Kuo tradition of landscape painting in China, which An Kyŏn helped make one of the most popular among painters during the early Yi period. These four album leaves belong to that tradition, as it had been interpreted by later artists of the Chin (1115-1234 A.D.), Yüan (1279-1368 A.D.) and particularly the early Ming (15th and early 16th centuries) Dynasties. Such post-Sung interpretations are characterized by thick, undulating contour lines, flattened forms, the closing off of space and the combination of prominent narrative elements with monumental landscape forms.

In comparison to An Kyŏn's *Dream Journey to Peach Blossom Spring* of 1447 A.D. (now in the Tenri University Library in Nara, Japan), the authenticity of which is uncontested, these album leaves are more conservative and less original. They may have been done by a contemporary of An's who followed the Li-Kuo School style more closely.

182. Four Goats
Anonymous, probably early Yi (15th or 16th century A.D.)
Fragment of a handscroll mounted as an album leaf, ink and colors on silk
H. 33.4 cm
National Museum of Korea

This is probably a fragment of a larger work. A painting of sheep in the National Museum of Korea, similar in style and technique, seems to be a second fragment of the same work.

In this painting the four goats, two by two, head toward the right. The viewer is immediately struck by the extremely fine lines of ink and opaque white pigment which depict the goats' hair. This technique is similar to that used in Chinese Southern Sung (1127-1279 A.D.) Academy animal paintings. Here, however, there is only a minimal sense of three-dimensionality, achieved by highlighted areas along the contours of the black goat and on the ridges extending from the animal's forehead. Nevertheless, the artist successfully captured the natural movement of the goats. In contrast to the fine brushwork used for the animals, the background rocks are rendered in dark, bold brushstrokes.

Compared with Kim Tu-ryang's painting of a dog (see No. 222), the goats appear much less realistic and three-dimensional. This difference suggests that *Goats* predates *A Dog Scratching*, perhaps by a century or two.

183. A Dog and Puppies
By Yi Am (1499 - after 1545 A.D.)
Yi, Hanging scroll, ink and light colors on paper
H. 73 cm
National Museum of Korea

Beneath a tree a mother dog suckles her puppies. The artist paid no particular attention to naturalistic features of the dogs, such as their fur, but instead treated them as a group in broad areas of dark and light. In fact, the only truly colorful accent in this essentially monochromatic composition is provided by the mother dog's red bell collar. The scroll is unsigned but bears a seal which reads Chŏngjung, the artist's style name.

The theme of animals in a peaceful, secure environment was popular during the Southern Sung Dynasty (1127-1279 A.D.) in China, particularly among court painters. Yi Am's animal paintings were said to have been based on the works of such painters, particularly those of the court painter

Mao I (active 1165-1173 A.D.), although more direct inspiration probably came from early Ming (15th and early 16th centuries A.D.) paintings of such themes.

A member of the royal family, Yi Am was known for his paintings of animals, insects and birds and flowers. In Japan he was long mistaken for a Japanese monk-painter active in the Muromachi period (1392-1573 A.D.), probably because a number of his paintings taken to Japan bear the seal "Wan-san Chŏngjung," once interpreted as a Japanese Buddhist name. This view was corrected when it was learned that Chŏngjung was a name used by Yi Am, and Wansan the region from which he came.

184. A Bull
By Kim Che (born after 1509 A.D.)
Yi
Album leaf, ink and light colors on paper
H. 26.3 cm
Seoul National University Museum

A heavy and powerful-looking bull is placed beneath an overhanging rock whose diagonal thrust echoes the direction of the animal's movement. The bull is painted in bold contrasts of light and dark with no attention to fine detail, a style similar to that of the preceding scroll, *Dog and Puppies* (No. 183).

In China, bucolic scenes of herdboys and water buffaloes were frequently painted by Southern Sung Academy painters such as Li T'ang (ca. 1050 - 1130 A.D.) and Li Ti (1100 - after 1197 A.D.). In the early Yüan period (1279 - 1368 A.D.) this tradition was continued by Mao Lun (late 13th - early 14th century A.D.) and Chang Fang-ju (14th century A.D.). Kim Che's rendition, however, is reminiscent of the work of early Ming (15th and early 16th centuries A.D.) professional painters in both brushwork and composition, although the posture of the bull, with its back toward the viewer, is not typical.

Kim Che, also known by his artist name of Yangsong-dang (here his sobriquet, or pen name—*hao* in Chinese), came from an illustrious family of scholars. He chose, however, to devote his life to painting and never bothered to take the official examinations. Nevertheless, at some point he did serve as a minor official in the government. Apparently he was considered the best painter of his time, for his excellence in painting and calligraphy often is compared with that of Ch'oe Yip (1539 - 1632 A.D.) and Han Sŏk-pong (1543 - 1605 A.D.). He is said to have excelled in all subject matter, including animals. His interest in painting oxen was continued by his grandnephew Kim Sik, also represented in this exhibition (see No. 195).

185 a-b. Landscapes
By Hoeŭn (ca. 16th century A.D.)
Yi
Two album leaves, ink on silk
H. 19.8 cm (each)
National Museum of Korea

The first leaf (No. 185a) is a landscape in which a scholar, accompanied by his boy servant, heads toward a cottage surrounded by a bamboo grove and a few old trees. A band of mist separates these middle ground elements from the mountains in the background. To the right of the cottage is a small waterfall, suggesting that the season is early spring before the stream has swollen. Scanty foliage on the trees and choppy vegetation on top of the mountains also indicate that season. In the second leaf (No. 185b) a lone fisherman sits by the edge of the water in the foreground. Again, a band of floating mist blurs the space between the foreground and background mountains, which are slightly more jagged than those in the first leaf. The compositions of both album leaves, with horizontal vistas fading into the distance, seem more appropriate for a handscroll format and may, in fact, have been based on that of a handscroll.

Stylistically these two paintings belong to the late 15th or early 16th century, when Li-Kuo style landscape painting became popular in Korea. Some of the features that distinguish these album leaves as Li-Kuo style paintings are: the strong calligraphic brushstrokes which define the mountains and tree trunks; the soft ink washes which impart an eroded appearance to the mountains; and the "crab-claw" strokes which define the twigs of trees, so named because the hook-like strokes resemble a crab's claw.

Nothing is known about the artist, Hoeŭn, who is identified by his seal as the painter of these two album leaves.

186. Landscape
Attributed to Yi Kyŏng-yun (1545 A.D. - ?)
Yi, Hanging scroll, ink and light colors on silk
H. 91.1 cm
National Museum of Korea

This hanging scroll attributed to Yi Kyŏng-yun consists of a mountain landscape with scholars and their attendants in the middle ground. A leafy branch forms an arch over a lone crane and one of the seated figures. A band of mist which extends horizontally across the width of the scroll separates the middle ground from the distant hills. This painting loosely follows the compositional schema of many Chinese Che School paintings of the 15th and 16th centuries, although the vertical accent tends to be more prominent in the Chinese examples. Despite its relatively large size, the painting lacks a sense of monumentality. This is the result of the artist's peculiar manner of rendering mountains and cliffs: they are broken into series of flat overlapping light and dark areas which convey only a minimal sense of three-dimensionality.

Yi Kyŏng-yun was one of the best representatives of late 16th century "Korean Che School" landscape painters.

187 a-b. A Scholar Washing His Feet and Two Scholars Conversing About Wild Geese
Attributed to Yi Kyŏng-yun (1545 A.D. - ?)
Yi, Two album leaves, ink on silk
H. 31.2 cm (each)
Koryŏ University Museum

Broad areas of wash and thick drapery lines characterize figures and landscape settings in these two album leaves. The bold, fluent brushwork is in the manner of late 15th and early 16th century professional painters of China.

Works attributed to Yi Kyŏng-yun are best understood within the context of the 16th century "Korean Che School." In a pioneering article entitled "A Study of Korean Che School Painting," Professor Ahn Hwi-Joon coined this term to distinguish this type of Korean painting, in vogue from the 15th century on, from the Chinese Che School painting on which it was based. The painters belonging to the Che School in Ming China were predominantly professionals, while in Korea the Che School style was practiced by scholar-painters as well. This is because the Che School painting style, then current in the Chinese capital, was the one to which most of the scholar-painters of Yi Korea were exposed when they were sent to China as envoys.

188. Bamboo in the Wind
By Yi Chŏng (1541 - 1622 A.D.)
Yi
Hanging scroll, ink on silk
H. 127.7 cm
Kansong Museum of Fine Arts

In this bamboo painting Yi Chŏng used two different ink tones to create an illusion of depth as well as a contrasting pattern on the surface of the picture plane. The effect of the wind is conveyed by the sharp bend of the bamboo stalks toward the right. In the foreground rock Yi Chŏng interjects the kind of pronounced shading typical of the Che School in China. The artist signed the painting with his sobriquet, T'anŭn, in the upper right corner.

Ink bamboo painting seems to have been practiced widely among scholar-painters of the Koryŏ Dynasty. The famous statesman and historian Kim Pu-sik (1075 - 1151 A.D.) and the noted scholar and diplomat Yi Che-hyŏn (1287 - 1365 A.D.) are said to have excelled in this genre, although none of their works is extant today.

Ink bamboo painting first became popular in China among the scholar-painters of the Northern Sung period (960 - 1124 A.D.). It was considered the supreme vehicle of self-expression because of its technical affinity to calligraphy and because of the symbolic correlation of bamboo to the "Superior Man." Bamboo traditionally was associated with ideal Confucian virtues—solidity and strength, which enable the bamboo to withstand the harshness of nature, and flexibility, which allows it to bend but not break. Yi Chŏng's bamboo painting is said to have captured the spirit of that of Su Shih (1037 - 1101 A.D.), famous Northern Sung poet, statesman and scholar, and the likeness of that of the Northern Sung scholar-artist Wen T'ung (d. 1079 A.D.).

Yi Chŏng, also known by his princely title Sŏg'yang-kun, was the most famous ink bamboo painter of the middle Yi period. He excelled in poetry, calligraphy and painting. His devotion to brush and ink was so great that he continued to paint even after he lost his right arm during the Hideyoshi invasion of Korea in 1597. Since his earlier works were lost during the invasion, all his extant paintings presumably were done with his left hand.

189. Bamboo
By Yi Chŏng (1541 - 1622 A.D.)
Yi, Hanging scroll, ink on silk
H. 148.8 cm
Dongwon Museum of Fine Arts

This painting, signed T'anŭn, Yi Chŏng's sobriquet, in the upper right corner, is different from Yi Chŏng's bamboo painting in the Kansong Museum (No. 188) in its more naturalistic description of that plant. Two sturdy stalks of bamboo are shown growing out of a round earthen mound and rendered with pronounced shading to emphasize the roundness of the stalks. The crescent of dark ink placed at each joint reinforces its cylindrical shape. This technique has been called the "dark ink joint technique." The bamboo leaves were done with the brush held slanted, thus exposing the tip. The same technique, used for the clerical script (li shu) in calligraphy, allows greater modulation of the strokes and consequently more expressive quality. In this painting the leaves appear battered by weather and age, as is appropriate for such thick stalks. This painting justifies the admiration shown for the life-like quality of Yi Chŏng's bamboo by one of his contemporaries: "Now I wonder whether the bamboo has turned into black ink or the black ink into bamboo."

Some of the Chinese precedents for this kind of naturalistic rendering of bamboo include works by Wen T'ung (d. 1079 A.D.) and Li K'an (1245 - 1320 A.D.). These two painters, however, did not employ the "dark ink joint technique." The joints on their bamboo are simply accentuated with additional layers of ink. By Yi Chŏng's time, however, Korean ink bamboo painters were in contact with the works of early Ming painters. Yi Chŏng himself was said to have followed Hsia Ch'ang (1388 - 1470 A.D.) and Chu Tuan (a follower of Hsia Ch'ang, active at the Ming court, 1506 - 1521 A.D.), who both used the "dark ink joint technique."

190 a-b. Autumn Moon Over Tung-t'ing Lake and Night Rain on the Hsiao and Hsiang Rivers
Attributed to Kim Myŏng-guk (1600 - after 1662 A.D.)

Yi, Two album leaves, ink on paper
H. 29.3 cm (each)
Namgung Ryun Collection

These are two in a series of "Eight Views of the Hsiao and Hsiang Rivers," in Hunan Province in South China. The first leaf describes the mist-laden atmosphere over Lake Tung-t'ing with a rising full moon above the mountains. In the second leaf two figures make their way along the rain-drenched river against the strong wind. Dark, heavy ink lines define the river bank, rocks and trees in the foreground. Large axe-cut texture strokes with strongly contrasting shading on the foreground rock in No. 190b clearly indicate the artist's preference for the Chinese Che School style. However, the mountains and rivers in the background are handled with soft ink tones to provide a greater sense of spatial depth. Although neither album leaf is signed by Kim Myŏng-guk, the quality of the work suggests an artist of Kim's caliber.

The "Eight Views" as a collective theme in landscape painting became popular in China during the Northern Sung period (960 - 1127 A.D.). Although tradition credits Sung Ti (965 - 1043 A.D.) as the first to paint this theme, it might have begun even earlier. Literary sources indicate that the "Eight Views" was introduced into Korea as early as the 12th century. King Myŏngjong (reigned 1171 - 1197 A.D.) of the Koryŏ Dynasty is said to have ordered scholars to compose poems on the theme and had his favorite painter, Yi Kwang-p'il, paint them. In China, Sung painters seem to have favored the handscroll format in depicting the "Eight Views," although Ming and later artists also used album or hanging scroll formats. In some cases, the scenes were depicted on eight or four-panel screens. Most extant examples from Korea and Japan belong to the latter category.

Kim Myŏng-guk was one of the leading members of the Painting Bureau during the mid 17th century. According to his biography he had a great sense of humor and an enormous capacity for drink. Twice he accompanied the Official Messenger to Japan: first in 1636 and again in 1643. He was famous for landscape and figure paintings in the Ming Che School style, which flourished in Korea from the early 16th century on. He also was one of the few painters in Korea who dealt with Ch'an (pronounced *Sŏn* in Korean) Buddhist themes in the Southern Sung Ch'an painting style.

191 a-b. A Strolling Scholar *and* A Gentleman on a Donkey
By Kim Myŏng-guk (1600 - after 1662 A.D.)
Yi, Two album leaves, ink on paper
H. 29.3 cm (each)
Namgung Ryun Collection

Kim Myŏng-guk's fame as a figure painter, mentioned in the preceding entry, is supported by these two figure paintings. In No. 191a, a scholar in Chinese dress holding a long bamboo walking staff stands at the edge of a cliff under a diagonally thrusting rock. No. 191b depicts a traveling gentleman in a traditional Korean costume complete with *kat* (high hat) and *chumŏni* (purse), which hangs down from his belt. The donkey and man are painted with quick, fluid brushstrokes which provide a sense of swift movement. The ground plane is simply defined by a light horizontal stroke. There are no clearly distinguishable brushstrokes in the background except for freely applied dabs of ink merely suggesting the foliage there. In the upper corner of No. 191a appear both the signature "Yŏndam" (the artist's sobriquet) and the artist's seal. No. 191b has a seal only, reading "Yŏndam," in the corresponding corner.

Although the themes of these leaves are not specifically Ch'an Buddhist ones, the artist employed the bold abbreviated brushwork which he frequently used in his paintings of Ch'an Buddhist subjects. No. 191a is particularly close to some of the figure paintings by Liang K'ai (active first half

of the 13th century A.D.), a Chinese Southern Sung painter who left the Academy to devote himself to Ch'an Buddhism.

Kim's cursive style of painting exhibited here evidently was carried to an extreme in the ink-splash paintings the artist purportedly did for the samurai of Japan during the two visits he made to that country, in 1636 and 1643. It also suggests that Kim Myŏng-guk may have followed the pattern set by Chinese painters of the 15th and early 16th centuries who adopted bold and spontaneous painting styles and affected eccentricities in their personal habits.

192 a-c. Landscapes
By Yun Ŭi-rip (1568 - 1643 A.D.)
Yi, Three album leaves, ink and light colors on silk
H. 21.5 cm (each)
National Museum of Korea

These three landscapes are from a set of eight album leaves now in the National Museum of Korea. The first leaf depicts a broad stream fed by a waterfall cascading down the huge rocky cliff. Beyond the cliff are distant mountains and a few cottages nestled in the woods. A boulder with two large overhanging trees in the foreground serves as a *repoussoir*. Three travelers and a donkey are heading toward the right on the bridge immediately behind the boulder. It is a scene of early summer: the stream is full and vegetation has begun to grow. In both this scene and the spring scene (leaf C), with its drooping willow branches, Yun Ŭi-rip appropriately chose the Che School style to depict the bold facets of the rocks. Sweeping strokes of dark ink and strong highlights are employed effectively. As the river recedes in the distance, a soft mist bathes the scenery, giving spatial depth.

The second leaf is a winter scene with mountains and a river. Here, Yun Ŭi-rip employed the Li-Kuo style, whose soft and undulating lines are suitable for the soft, snow-covered mountains. In the lower left are a group of bare trees and a pavilion on a promontory above the trees. Two fishing boats are moored on the icy water, but a lone fisherman is still out on the river. Distant mountains are summarily treated with a few dots representing winter vegetation. Although one may classify such a painting in the Li-Kuo tradition, the simple strokes of the foreground trees deviate considerably from the gnarled, "crab-clawed" trees that are the hallmark of the Li-Kuo style. Yun Ŭi-rip seems to have preferred blunt strokes for his trees and foliage. Scholar-painters of the early Yi period who adopted Chinese painting styles, be it the Li-Kuo or the Che, did so selectively, and created styles uniquely their own.

The four characters "Wŏldam nongmuk," or "Wŏldam (the artist's sobriquet) Playfully Painted It," appear in red against the dark overcast wintry sky.

Yun Ŭi-rip was a scholar-painter of the early Yi period. He passed the metropolitan official examination in 1594, and his long career as an official culminated in his post as President of the Board of Rites. Like many other scholar-painters of the early Yi period, Yun Ŭi-rip painted in both the Li-Kuo style of the late Yüan period (14th century A.D.) and the Ma-Hsia style as modified by early Ming painters of the Che School. Together with his brother Chŏng-rip (1571 - 1627 A.D.), who was also a high government official, Ŭi-rip was one of the most important figures in the development of the Che School painting style in Korea (See Nos. 186 and 187 for more information on the "Korean Che School").

193. Portrait of Yi Hang-bok (1556 - 1618 A.D.)
Anonymous, Yi (early 17th century A.D.)
Album leaf, ink and colors on paper
H. 59.35 cm
Seoul National University Museum

This is one of the few surviving early examples of Yi Dynasty portraiture. The face is depicted with great care and detail while the costume is only roughly sketched in.

Fine lines and subtle shading describe the subject's facial features. If this is a posthumous portrait, or one done late in Yi Hang-bok's life, his anxious expression may refer to the troubles which he encountered and which led to his exile to a remote area in the north, where he died. He wears an official robe and *samo* hat with two wings *(kat)*, the kind worn by the three highest-ranking ministers.

Yi Hang-bok was a 16th century scholar-official descended from the family of the reknown scholar-official Yi Che-hyŏn (1287 - 1367 A.D.) of the late Koryŏ Dynasty. He passed the government examinations at the age of twenty-four and gradually rose to the highest official rank, that of Yŏngŭijŏng, equivalent to Chief State Councilor. He escorted King Sŏnjo (reigned 1568 - 1608 A.D.) during the royal flight north at the time of the Hideyoshi invasion, in 1592, and later successfully brought in the Ming armies of China to rescue Korea.

During the Yi Dynasty portraiture became a popular painting genre, and court painters frequently executed portraits of royal families, high officials and scholars. A commission to paint a royal portrait was the highest honor a professional court painter could receive. Portrait painting also was highly esteemed by upper class families, who made use of such paintings in their ancestor worship.

194. A Fisherman and Woodcutter (See Colorplate XXXIV)
Yi, By Yi Myŏng-uk (late 17th century A.D.)
Hanging scroll, ink and light colors on paper
H. 172.7 cm
Kansong Museum of Fine Arts

This large painting portrays a fisherman and a woodcutter on their way home, both carrying the tools of their trade. They converse with each other, gesturing in a lively manner. The fisherman's face is especially notable for its fine portrait-like quality. The artist employed delicate lines to model the contours of his face, framed by beard and mustache. In contrast to the delicate facial delineations, drapery lines are thick and jagged, a characteristic feature of Che School figure painting. The vitality of the picture derives not only from the lively expressions of the figures, but also from the sharp angular drapery lines and the wind-blown reeds scattered in the foreground and behind the figures.

Yi Myŏng-uk, a court painter during the reign of King Sukchong (reigned 1675 - 1720 A.D.), was famous for his figure paintings. He is said to have followed the figure styles of the early Ch'ing court painter Meng Yung-kuang (active 1650 - 1700 A.D.), who went to Korea and served as a court painter in Sukchong's Painting Bureau.

195. A Swimming Duck
Anonymous, Yi (ca. 17th century A.D.)
Album leaf, ink on paper
H. 66.6 cm
Namgung Ryun Collection

This album leaf depicts a duck swimming in a rapid swirl of water in an unusual bird's-eye view. The boldly outlined overhanging rocks above and the rapidly drawn water plants below create a tonal balance. A waterfall ripples over the rocks and into the center of the painting. The description of the duck is not as detailed as that of other animals painted by professional artists (see Nos. 196 and 197). But the unusual viewpoint does reveal a genuine creativity on the part of this anonymous painter. Both this album leaf and a similar hanging scroll by the 19th century painter Hong Se-sŏp (see No. 249) have a dynamic quality not often encountered in Chinese or Japanese paintings.

This painting is sometimes attributed to the 17th century scholar-painter Kim Sik, grandnephew of Kim Che (No. 184).

196. Cats and Sparrows
By Pyŏn Sang-byŏk (18th century A.D.)

Yi
Hanging scroll, ink and light colors on silk
H. 93.7 cm
National Museum of Korea

Signed with the artist's sobriquet Hwa-jae, this scroll is one of the livelier animal paintings executed in Korea. A playful cat stops scrambling up an old tree in response to his companion's meowing, while surprised little sparrows clamor on the branches above. The composition is well-organized, and the birds and cats are drawn with meticulous detail, in contrast to the more fluid treatment of the tree.

Pyŏn Sang-byŏk was a court painter who excelled in cats and fowl. He also was adept at portraiture and painted the portraits of more than one hundred officials. It was his enthusiasm for painting cats, however, which earned him the nickname Pyŏn Koyang or Pyŏn the Cat.

197. Hens and Chickens
By Pyŏn Sang-byŏk (18th century A.D.)
Yi
Hanging scroll, ink and light colors on silk
H. 94.4 cm
National Museum of Korea

This scroll is representative of Pyŏn Sang-byŏk's paintings of fowl. Here a hen is feeding her chicks an insect which she holds in her beak. The painter presents them in a pleasant, peaceful setting, near a garden rock, and enlivens the scene with butterflies and bees buzzing around briar flowers. As in the preceding scroll, the artist's handling of the main subject is different from his handling of the setting. The meticulous depiction of the hen and chicks stands out in contrast to the more generalized description of the rock with flat washes of ink.

198. Jar   (See Colorplate XXXI)
White porcelain with underglaze iron decoration
Yi (17th century A.D.)
H. 53.2 cm
Ewha Woman's University Museum

Regarded by some as the largest and best of its type, this jar with grape clusters hanging on vines is representative of ceramics produced at a government kiln site in Kwangju in the 17th century. The shape has the typical middle Yi Dynasty form with straight vertical neck and extravagantly wide, flaring shoulder diminishing in a curve to a flat base. The glaze also is of very high quality, being pure white rather than bluish white.

Numerous kilns all over Korea produced iron-painted wares. Some of the technically superior examples were made at official kilns in Kwangju and at kiln sites around Seoul. During the middle Yi, underglaze iron decoration became highly abstract, especially at provincial kilns. By contrast, government kilns maintained realistic styles. Judging from the deft handling of the brush and the pictorial ambiance of natural forms drifting in space, it is likely the painting of this jar was executed by an official artist.

199. Bottle
White porcelain with underglaze blue decoration
Yi (late 17th century A.D.)
H. 27.5 cm
National Museum of Korea

With its sparse use of blue, this octagonal wine vessel reflects an artisan's skill in maximizing the use of rare cobalt. Flowering plants and bamboo decorate opposite sides of the body. The flowers resemble chrysanthemums while the leaves suggest orchids. The images are an interesting combination of diluted tones and stronger blues, so that some motifs appear indefinite and vague while others, such as the bamboo, are more lucidly defined and sharply focused. Because of this great capacity for suggestion, the brushwork is highly expressive. The clay is pure white, and the milky white glaze with light bluish tinge is transparent.

200. Jar   White porcelain
Yi (17th - 18th century A.D.)
H. 42.7 cm
National Museum of Korea

Impressive in its large size, this asymmetrical storage jar is made of two major sections luted together (the lute-joint is still noticeable). The mouth and foot were added separately.

From early to late Yi, the production of plain white porcelains was widespread from north to south (see Nos. 168, 209-211).

Large jars such as this are distinctively Korean in the sculptural simplicity of their robust, pure forms, allowing full attention to the irregular body and "hidden" beauty of the bluish-toned glaze.

201. Bottle
White porcelain with underglaze blue, copper and iron decoration
Yi (17th - 18th century A.D.)
H. 41.6 cm
Kansong Museum of Fine Arts

A number of Korean porcelains are painted colorfully with underglaze blue and copper, but this tall-necked bottle is among the relative few that also are decorated with a third pigment, underglaze iron. There is an almost "precious," artificial quality to the chrysanthemums, orchids, honey bees and butterflies on the body which are embellished further by being in relief.

The chrysanthemum leaves and bees were painted in underglaze iron. Some chrysanthemum petals were left white while others were decorated with copper oxide. The orchids were brushed with cobalt blue. The butterflies and bees stand out in iron and copper.

The bottle is allegedly from the Kaesŏng area, but the high quality of the glaze and clay indicate it must have been made in Kwangju at the central government kiln site which supplied the royal household with ceramics.

202. Brush Stand
White porcelain with underglaze blue decoration
Yi (18th century A.D.)
H. 16 cm
Hoam Art Museum

This narrow cylindrical brush stand is sparingly decorated with underglaze blue. A straight line drawn above the base provides a ground line for orchids on one side, and plum, bamboo and orchids on the other. The soft dreamy quality of the painting, the gentle reticence and economy of brushwork, the evanescent tones of diluted and suffusing blue—all create a mood distinctively Korean (see also No. 199). Long prized by Japanese connoisseurs, this kind of imagery has been called "autumn grasses" and admired for its exquisitely sensitive and serene qualities.

203. Bottle   (See Colorplate XXXII)
White porcelain with underglaze blue decoration
Yi (late 18th century A.D.)
H. 35 cm
Hong Du-yong Collection

Faceted bottles such as this were produced in sizeable numbers from the late 17th to the mid 18th centuries (see also No. 199). This example has the somewhat shorter neck and plump body characteristic of later 18th century products. The quality of the glaze and luster of the blue are also typical of porcelains made after the mid 18th century.

Porcelains of this period typically have decoration zones marked by single or double lines on the lower part of the body. Separated from the base by lines encircling the body, the main decoration consists of bamboo plants and a plum tree painted on opposite sides of the jar. The ground line conveys the effect of scattered vegetation.

204. Jar
White porcelain with underglaze blue decoration
Yi (18th century A.D.)
H. 38.1 cm
National Museum of Korea

This jar exhibits a typical 18th century shape with its swollen shoulder, upright mouth and tapering waist.

Popular during the period was the use of pictures, vignettes of famous themes, or entire landscapes, as decoration for the bodies of vessels (see for example No. 205). Two cartouches on either side of this jar contain separate landscapes enclosed in double lines. A plum and bamboo are arranged in the plain areas between the "windows" of landscapes. The painting is skillfully done, as if by a professional painter. A transparent glaze is applied evenly over the white body.

205. Vase
White porcelain with underglaze blue decoration
Yi (mid 18th century A.D.)
H. 32 cm
Hoam Art Museum

This footless vase was fired on silicate grit supports. The ovoid body with everted mouth is decorated with landscapes, perhaps scenes of the Hsiao and Hsiang Rivers in China (a theme illustrated in No. 190). The accomplished rendering of cliffs, trees and long grass, boats, and distant mountains; the interplay between brushstrokes, paler washes and long stretches of blank space; and the development of recession from foreground to distance—all indicate that the painting was not executed by an ordinary potter.

This object is considered to be a rare mid-18th century product of the government kiln at Kŭmsa-ri in Kwangju.

206. Jar
White porcelain with underglaze copper decoration
Yi (late 18th century A.D.)
H. 27.8 cm
National Museum of Korea

This round jar is close to folk art in its relaxed, unpretentious beauty. Certain technical faults, such as the irregular shape, crawling glaze, impure glaze color and fingernail marks, suggest that the piece was made hastily, for it did not require the perfection of potting and glazing necessary for court wares. Very sophisticated, however, are the abstractions of line and form which develop out of such recognizable motifs as grape leaves and vine tendrils, painted in copper oxide around the upper portion of the body.

A number of similar vessels painted with grapevines, lotus, chrysanthemums and birds have come to light, suggesting that one local kiln may have specialized in this type for a certain period of time. However, the precise location of the kiln has not yet been clearly established. The similarities with other jars include the round shape, with belly wider than shoulder, the double rings under the mouth, the grayish cast to the glaze, and the two tones of reddish brown and lighter, brighter red in the underglaze copper designs.

207. Water-Dropper
White porcelain with underglaze blue and copper decoration
Yi (18th century A.D.)
H. 4.8 cm
National Museum of Korea

Water-droppers in the shape of mythical beasts are generally larger than this one which is so small it can be held in the palm of the hand. Certain elements such as the "mane," tail and haunches are painted with underglaze blue and copper. Sometimes identified as a sea creature capable of exhaling large quantities of water and therefore supposedly used as a charm against fire on the gates of Yi palace architecture, this fantastic beast has a hole in the mouth and on the back for the filling and emitting of water.

208. Water-Dropper   (See Colorplate XXXIII)
White porcelain with underglaze blue and copper decoration
Yi (late 18th century A.D.)
H. 10.3 cm
Hoam Art Museum

This fine, white porcelain peach-shaped water-dropper is carved, incised and colored with delightful naturalistic details. A twig of a peach tree painted in underglaze copper acts as the base. It is hollowed out and sculptured to resemble twisted knots and tiny shoots springing from a branch. Another edge of the twig acts as a foil for the spout. Two finely veined leaves and an insect complete the decoration. They appear in relief and are painted in blue pigments.

209. Pitcher with Cover   White porcelain
Yi (19th century A.D.)
H. 27.8 cm
National Museum of Korea

An exceptionally good piece from the government kiln, this "pitcher" is in fact a container for boiled herb medicine used in the royal household. A very ingenious but simple mechanism was added to prevent poison from being put into the pitcher. The lid fits deep into the neck of the pitcher and is held in place by a bronze wire bored through each side of the neck. Originally the wire would have extended out to the spout, where a metal "plug" would have been inserted. The lid would have been padlocked by the metal wire, and thus made secure against tampering. The glassy glaze is typical of late Yi examples (compare No. 168).

210. Water-Dropper   White porcelain
Yi (19th century A.D.)
H. 11.1 cm
National Museum of Korea

Because of its shape, this type of object is known in Korea by the colloquial term of "kneecap water-dropper." Water is poured in and drained out through the loop-shaped spout attached to the shoulder. The flow of water is stopped by pressing a finger on the air hole on top.
   This luminous white porcelain is believed to be a product of the government kilns established since 1752 at Punwŏn-ni on the banks of the Han River, where they could be easily supplied by river transport with clay and fuel from outlying areas.

211. Brush Stand
White porcelain with openwork decoration
Yi (19th century A.D.)
H. 12.4 cm
Hoam Art Museum

Miniature white porcelain objects, such as stands for holding writing brushes, enjoyed great popularity during the 18th and 19th centuries. This brush stand is divided into sections: a twisted rope band for the mouth-rim; an interconnected series of openwork rings, brackets and cross-supports for the mid zone; and interlocking lozenges for the slightly narrower lower part. On the base is engraved a Chinese character meaning "great." The bluish white glaze is thick and has no crackles.
   Because of its technical virtuosity, this item is believed to be a work of the government kiln in Punwŏn-ni.

212. Water-Dropper
White porcelain with underglaze copper decoration
Yi (19th century A.D.)
H. 5.2 cm
National Museum of Korea

It was during the Koryŏ period that Korean ceramics first were decorated with underglaze copper (see Nos. 145-152), but in Yi the technique was never used to the extent of underglaze blue or iron. This water-dropper is unusual in that the whole body is painted in underglaze copper, except for two cranes which remain in reserve in pure white and stand out in low relief against a reddish background. The bottom edges of the piece are cut with ogival arches.

213. Bowl
White porcelain with underglaze blue decoration
Yi (19th century A.D.)
H. 10.5 cm
National Museum of Korea

This kind of bowl is called *p'unju* ("flat bowl") in Korean and was used to serve a cool juice mixed with fruits (*hwach'ae*) similar to a punch. A large Chinese character meaning "good fortune" is written on the bottom of the bowl, and two Chinese characters meaning "bat" are painted on the outside. Flying bats cover the exterior of the bowl, illustrating the Chinese pun whereby "bat" (*fu*) and "good fortune" (*fu*) are associated, thereby making the bat a symbol of good luck. These symbols were used as decorative motifs during the late Yi Dynasty and are still auspicious.

214. Water-Dropper
White porcelain with underglaze blue decoration
Yi (early 19th century A.D.)
H. 7.1 cm
National Museum of Korea

The sharp angles of this box-shaped water-dropper are matched by the indented recessions around the base and the spiky angular drawing of bamboo, leaves and other plants on the sides. The motifs are given diluted washes of blue, and a light bluish glaze covers the body.

215. Dish
White porcelain with underglaze blue decoration
Yi (19th century A.D.)
H. 1.9 cm
National Museum of Korea

This dish is unusually thin and is delicately painted with carefully drawn and textured motifs filled with washes of blue. The composition has a lyric charm that is curiously offset by the presence of more eccentric elements. Wild plum blossoms are set impressionistically against a blurred, speckled background around the inner rim. The central area is devoted to a plantain, strange convoluted rock formations, a tea kettle and a brazier, along with orchid leaves and Chinese pinks. A rabbit stares from one side, and his rather human face adds an amusing, but slightly unsettling note. The light, bluish-toned glaze has been applied relatively thickly.

216. Dish
White porcelain with underglaze blue decoration
Yi (19th century A.D.)
H. 4 cm
National Museum of Korea

This is a typical shape for utilitarian dishes of the late 18th and 19th centuries. The mouth is slightly everted, the dish wall thick, and the base also thick and wide. The half circle at the top of the painted interior looks either like a sun or moon. Below this are a range of high mountains, before which birds fly over an aquatic expanse. Three fish swim downward in a setting lush with plants, hemmed in by rock formations. The thick glaze has a light bluish cast.

217. Dish
White porcelain with underglaze blue decoration
Yi (19th century A.D.)
H. 2.8 cm
National Museum of Korea

While dishes are most commonly round, this one is rectangular and belongs to a type produced in the 18th and 19th centuries for everyday usage for the highest echelons of society. It is even thinner than other top quality round dishes and probably belonged to the royal household or to a member of the aristocracy. The inner rim is decorated with an interlocking double keyfret pattern, and the interior is painted with a whimsical and highly stylized composition of pines growing from fingers of fantastic rocks. There is a positive and negative use of white designs on blue, and dark blue and light blue motifs on white, so that the pine cones and rocks are decoratively trimmed with white. On the outside, the curved edges of the plate are banded by double lines and by trailing arabesques with rosette-like flowers.

218. Water-Dropper
White porcelain with underglaze blue decoration
Yi (19th century A.D.)
H. 9.1 cm
Hoam Art Museum

A "kneecap water-dropper" like No. 210, this example is decorated on the upper part only, leaving most of the body an unadorned, milky white color. A blossoming plum tree in underglaze blue branches from the loop spout on the side across the hole on top. A faintly bluish-toned glaze coats the entire surface. The foot is low and wide, which helps stabilize the circular shape.

219. Ch'ŏng-p'ung Valley   (See Colorplate XXXV)
By Chŏng Sŏn (1676 - 1759 A.D.)
Yi (dated 1739 A.D.)
Hanging scroll, ink and light colors on silk
H. 133.2 cm
Kansong Museum of Fine Arts

Among Chŏng Sŏn's depictions of the Ch'ŏng-p'ung (Cool Breeze) Valley, this is the largest one and the only example which bears a date. The kind of brushwork used in his painting of Mount Inwang (see No. 220), such as geometric areas of flat ink for rock cliffs and dotting for clumps of vegetation, is already apparent in this earlier work. Here, however, the vertical format of the hanging scroll is used to compress the landscape into a dense composition which is more formally and rigidly structured than that of his Mount Inwang painting. The dense composition may also be due to the artist's effort to be faithful to the actual appearance of the valley. A certain lack of coherent spatial relationships in this scroll is compensated for by vigorous brushwork which is characteristic of most of Chŏng Sŏn's work.

The painting is titled and signed by the artist with his well-known sobriquet, Kyŏmjae, and bears a date.

A study of Chŏng Sŏn's paintings reveals that he was familiar with both the professional and literati painting styles of Ming China. He seems to have started painting in the Che School manner, which was dominant in Korea until the late 17th century. Gradually he turned to literati styles, and became the most influential Korean artist in the development of literati taste in 18th century Yi painting. In *Ch'ŏngp'ung Valley* his attention to the formal construction of the landscape, broken down into almost abstract units separated by sharp bands of mist and level ground, and his pointedly disshevelled compositions are new to Korean painting. They set him apart from his predecessors while at the same time suggest that he was familiar with similar concerns in the works of the 17th century literati and indi-

vidualist masters of China.

One of the most celebrated and prolific painters of the late Yi Dynasty, Chŏng Sŏn was a member of the Painting Bureau and attained the rank of county magistrate *(hyŏn'gam)* in his late years. In addition to his role in the development of literati taste in Korean painting, he initiated a trend in landscapes known as *Chin'gyŏng sansu,* or "landscape painting of actual scenes," featuring well-known scenic spots of Korea. He traveled all over Korea in search of subjects for his landscape paintings, while most of his contemporaries relied on Chinese models for their inspiration. Some of his "true landscape" paintings include scenes of the Diamond Mountains and of areas in and around Seoul, such as the Ch'ŏngp'ung Valley, located on the eastern side of Mount Inwang.

220. Clear Skies Over Mount Inwang
By Chŏng Sŏn (1676 - 1759 A.D.)
Yi (dated 1751 A.D.)
Hanging scroll, ink and light colors on paper
H. 78.8 cm
Hoam Art Museum

Chŏng Sŏn did this painting of Mount Inwang, located to the northwest of Seoul, in 1751 at the age of 75. It is composed of three horizontal segments separated by bands of rising mist. Unlike the Ch'ŏngp'ung Valley composition (see No. 219) this one has a certain solidity and stability to it despite the opposing thrusts of trees and individual facets of the mountain's rocky surface.

The painting bears a title, date, artist's signature (Kyŏmjae), and two of his seals, reading Chŏng Sŏn and Wŏnbaek (another sobriquet).

221. Greeting Japanese Envoys in Tongnae
Attributed to Chŏng Sŏn (1676 - 1759 A.D.)
Yi, Folding screen, ink and colors on paper
H. 85 cm
National Museum of Korea

In this ten-panel folding screen attributed to Chŏng Sŏn, Korean officials receive Japanese envoys at Tongnae, now a part of Pusan, the southernmost port in Korea. In response to uncontrolled Japanese piracy, the Korean government appointed the feudal lord of Tsushima, in Japan, to handle official Korean-Japanese trade and in 1426 restricted the Japanese merchants in Korea to three ports, one of them the guarded quarter in Tongnae.

This screen is an important work not only for studying Chŏng Sŏn's "true landscape" painting but also for reconstructing the features of the area described. Villages, buildings, ports and mountains are mentioned by name, and buildings are faithfully recorded, as if from observation.

The screen opens at the right with the depiction of the walled city of Tongnae. A long procession leaves the South Gate of the citadel heading toward the Japanese settlement at Ch'oryang, known as Ch'oryang Waegwan. The procession includes the magistrate of Tongnae District, seated in a *kama* or palanquin (panel 4), flag-holding officials (panel 5) and courtesans (panel 6). In panel 7 the procession is shown entering the first gate of the Japanese enclave. Panel 8 depicts kneeling Japanese envoys, distinguishable by their hair styles, paying respect to the Royal Tablet, symbolic of the absent king. The last panel describes the banquet hall.

The screen does not bear a date, but can be placed within the period 1710-1758 A.D. on the basis of historical information on the building. Although the work is not signed by Chŏng Sŏn, his name does appear, along with the title, on the frame of the screen.

In the varied use of Mi dots and in the rendering of trees, the painting is similar to Chŏng Sŏn's more conservative works. The orderly arrangement of hills, trees, and shore areas, and the careful drawing of figures and architecture are all part of a detailed and descriptive approach appropriate to the subject matter. In fact, the screen may have been commissioned as a kind of official record.

In Korea folding screens were used as room dividers and, at the same time, provided large areas for painted decoration. They were also an excellent means of focusing attention on a specific area of the room and in this capacity were frequently displayed behind the ruler's throne.

222. A Dog Scratching
By Kim Tu-ryang (1696 - 1763 A.D.)
Yi, Album leaf, ink on paper
H. 23 cm
National Museum of Korea

This small album leaf depicts a dog scratching, in an almost unbelievably contorted posture and with a slightly smirking expression. The meticulous fine-line description of the fur and the attention to shading may be due to Western influence, entering Korea through Ch'ing China (1644 - 1911 A.D.). The roughly drawn branch and grass contrast sharply with this fine, detailed rendition.

A member of the Painting Bureau, Kim Tu-ryang painted animals as well as landscapes. In his landscape painting he worked in the Wu School literati tradition of Ming China. Both he and Chŏng Sŏn (see Nos. 219-221) helped initiate the literati phase of late Yi painting, and both were precocious in their interest in genre painting, fifty years before it began to flourish under the influence of artists such as Kim Hong-do and Sin Yun-bok.

223. Portrait of Yi Chae (1680 - 1746 A.D.)
Anonymous, Yi (probably 18th century A.D.)
Hanging scroll, ink and light colors on silk
H. 97 cm
National Museum of Korea

In this portrait, the Neo-Confucian scholar and painter Yi Chae is dressed in *hakch'ang-ŭi* and *pokkŏn*, or informal gown and soft cloth headpiece, worn by officials and gentry. The delicate drawing of the facial features and beard and the use of shading around the eyes and cheeks successfully capture the lifelike appearance of the old scholar. The dark, black color of the headpiece and the hems and band of the robe contrast strikingly with the softly drawn drapery folds of the white robe.

Yi Chae entered government service after passing the civil service examinations in 1702 and 1707. He attained several high official positions, including First Counselor (1717) and Second Minister of Rites (1721). Implicated in factional struggles, however, he withdrew from government to study Neo-Confucian philosophy. He returned to court in 1725 as Director of the Office of Special Counselors but withdrew again in 1727. He spent the rest of his life in Yong'in, not far south of Seoul, teaching Confucian philosophy. Some of his writings, including *Toam chip*, are still well known today.

224. Looking for Plum Blossoms
By Sim Sa-jŏng (1707 - 1769 A.D.)
Yi (dated 1766 A.D.)
Hanging scroll, ink and light colors on silk
H. 115 cm
National Museum of Korea

In this painting the foreground begins with a large boulder whose contours are defined by dark, heavy lines. Lighter texture strokes with a few dots create a spiraling motion which makes the boulder resemble a large conch shell. From here a large deciduous tree covered with snow extends far above the Pa Bridge. A scholar riding a donkey and his servant approach the bridge. The foreground and middle ground trees neatly frame this group of figures. Beyond the bridge rise several mountain peaks; that in the upper left thrusts diagonally toward the right and in its motion counterbalances the boulder in the foreground. The choppy brushstrokes representing vegetation on the mountain tops are reminiscent of those in late Ming winter landscapes, es-

pecially by Lan Ying (1585 - after 1660 A.D.), in the style of Fan K'uan (active early 11th century A.D.).

The subject of this painting is identified by the artist's inscription in the upper right corner as "Searching for Plum Blossoms at the Pa Bridge." The Pa Bridge (pronounced P'a in Korean) crosses the Pa River, a tributary of the Wei, in Shensi Province, north China, some 25 miles east of Ch'ang-an prefecture. The bridge has long been a favorite spot for seeing friends off and thus became known as the *hsiao hun ch'iao* or the "bridge where one parts with one's soul." Looking for the first plum blossoms of the year is a popular activity in early spring, often when the snow still covers the ground, since the wild plum is one of the first trees to bloom. It is one of the Three Friends of Winter, along with the pine and bamboo, and is associated with endurance and purity.

Sim Sa-jŏng, better known by his sobriquet Hyŏnjae, came from an illustrious family from Ch'ŏng-song. He is said to have begun painting at the age of five. Although his biographers inform us that Sim studied painting with Chŏng Sŏn (see Nos. 219 - 221), his paintings in general bear little resemblance to those of his teacher.

225. Viewing the Waterfall
By Yi In-sang (1710 - 1760 A.D.)
Yi, Fan painting mounted as hanging scroll, ink and light colors on paper
H. 23.8 cm
National Museum of Korea

An old contorted pine tree dominates the composition. Behind it a cascade plunging down the center of the picture serves as a backdrop. The sharply faceted rocks on the right are complemented by a similarly fractured rocky plateau on the left. It is from this vantage point that a seated scholar enjoys the view of the waterfall. The whirling pattern of the water beneath the waterfall is echoed in the curling clouds above the scholar. The artist's inscription reads:

The angry waterfall suddenly becomes chopsticks beyond the pine.
Floating clouds threaten to band together to cover the sun.
Painted on an autumn day south of Sohoro—for Pyŏngwi's fan.

Pine trees must have been Yi In-sang's favorite theme, for they appear time and again as the dominant element in his paintings. In China the pine, bamboo and prunus were grouped together as the "Three Friends", and became one of the favorite themes of scholar-painters from the late 13th century on.

Yi In-sang was a scholar-painter who passed the metropolitan civil service examination in 1745 and served as a county magistrate (*hyŏn'gam*). According to contemporary sources, he excelled in poetry, painting and calligraphy, especially the clerical script (*li-shu*) and seal script (*chuan-shu*). He also was a seal carver and collector of antiques. Most of his extant paintings show that he was a close follower of the Wu School painters of Ming China, particularly Shen Chou (1427 - 1509 A.D.) and Wen Cheng-ming (1470 - 1559 A.D.).

226. Listening to a Golden Oriole
By Kim Hong-do (1745 - after 1814 A.D.)
Yi, Hanging scroll, ink and light colors on paper
H. 117.1 cm
Kansong Museum of Fine Arts

An equestrian gentleman and his servant, traveling along a quiet river bank in spring, turn to watch a golden oriole singing on the willow branch. Kim Hong-do's use of delicate brushstrokes and light green color for the robe of the gentleman evokes the freshness of spring. The asymmetrical composition of the hanging scroll is well balanced by the poetic inscription and the artist's signature in the upper left.

The artist's inscription, signed with his sobriquet Tanwŏn, includes a seven-character quatrain by Yi Mun-uk describing the scenery with an elegant metaphor: the landscape is compared to a beautiful piece of silk being woven over the misty river by the movement of a golden shuttle, the yellow oriole. The inscription reads:

A beautiful woman under the flowers, a thousand birds (sing like) a reed organ.
Before a poet's wine jug, a pair of tangerines.
A yellow shuttle in confusion, willows on the bank.
They allure winds and mingle with rain, threads on the spring river.

The quatrain by Yi Mun-uk, a man of the Way (tao) in the Old Pine Hall,
Where the only sounds are those of chess playing and flowing water.

This painting is unusual among Kim Hong-do's works because its mood greatly depends on the poetic inscription.

227 a-b. Immortal and Crane and Chatting on the Southern Mountain

By Kim Hong-do (1745 - after 1814 A.D.)
Yi, Two album leaves, ink and light colors on paper
H. 29.4 cm (each)
Lee Hurak Collection

Both paintings illustrate Chinese poems of the T'ang Dynasty (618 - 906 A.D.) which the artist inscribed in the upper left corners. No. 227a illustrates a seven-character quatrain attributed to Lü Tung-pin (Lü Yen), an immortal worshipped in China as a titular god by the Ch'üan-chen sect of Northern Taoism from the Yüan Dynasty (1279 - 1368 A.D.) on. Here Lü Tung-pin is shown seated on top of the mountain. His attribute, a long sword, is slung across his back. Above him a crane flies toward the cliff on the right. According to Lü's biography, incised on a 13th century stele at Yung-lo-kung in Shansi Province, he learned the secrets of Taoism from the immortal Chung Li-ch'üan. For this reason, he often appears with a long sword. The poem which this leaf illustrates describes the flight ("drunken-dance") of the immortal to a mountain high above the sea where he gathers dewdrops to use in making the golden elixir of immortality:

Drunk, I dance and sing on the mountain above the sea.
At dawn, immortal dew drops round as cinnabar pills.
Night is deep, a crane flies away to the blue autumn sky.
The west wind blows from a myriad miles, chilling my sword.

No. 227b illustrates a five-character verse entitled "Retreat at Mount Chung-nan" by Wang Wei (699 - 759 A.D.), the famous Chinese T'ang Dynasty scholar-official and poet-painter. The poem describes a happy encounter between the poet, in his solitary wanderings around his retreat at the foot of Mount Chung-nan, and an "old man of the woods," a hermit or woodcutter. Kim paints these two figures with a few soft lines and dots. His simple rendition is in harmony with Wang Wei's poetic description of the mountainous setting, filled with mist and rising clouds. The "Southern Mountain" of the title refers to Mount Chungnan, a famous mountain situated to the south of Ch'ang-an, Shensi Province.

In addition to the poem by Lü Tung-pin, No. 227a bears a dedicatory inscription and a date corresponding to 1798. The inscription states that the album leaf was painted for a certain Pyŏn Ch'i-hwa. Since both leaves are similar in style and since both illustrate poems of a Taoist nature, it is possible that No. 227b also was painted for Mr. Pyŏn.

228 a-b. Wrestling Match and A Dancing Boy
(See Colorplate XXXVI)

By Kim Hong-do (1745 - after 1814 A.D.)
Yi, Two album leaves, ink and light colors on paper
H. 28 cm (each)
National Museum of Korea

The two album leaves shown here are from a ten-leaf album of genre paintings, now in the National Museum of Korea. No. 228a depicts two men wrestling, still a popular sport in Korea.

The struggling contestants are encircled by an enthusias-

tic audience. By his masterful use of simple lines and dots, the artist has conveyed a wide variety of facial expressions and gestures, thus imparting an air of animation and excitement to the painting. The artist included such details as a boy peddling sticks of sweets called *yŏt*.

No. 228b depicts a dancing youth and a group of musicians. Again the artist enlivens the genre scene with his observant descriptions of instruments and musicians, while capturing with his nervous, rhythmic line the energy of the dancing youth. The musical instruments shown here are from the top: *chwago*, a drum suspended from a beam and struck with a stick, *changu*, an hour-glass shaped drum used for popular music and festivals and beaten with the palm of the left hand and a stick held in the right hand, *p'iri*, a kind of bamboo flute, *taegŭm*, another kind of flute native to Korea, and *haegŭm*, a two-stringed fiddle.

It is interesting to note that the figures in each leaf are arranged in a circle without any indication of setting. Kim Hong-do's superb sense of composition seems to find its best expression in these simple figural arrangements. In keeping with the simplicity, his use of color is also restricted to light blue and light brown in the dancing scene and to a light tan in the wrestling scene.

The advent of genre painting in Korea at this time should be understood within the context of the contemporary social atmosphere in which *Sirhak* (practical learning) flourished among influential scholars such as Pak Chi-wŏn (1737 - 1805 A.D.). This movement resulted in an increased awareness of the importance of the common people, and for the first time the working-class was regarded as a worthwhile painting subject. Kim Hong-do's achievement in this field is often compared to that of Chŏng Sŏn (1676 - 1759 A.D.) in landscape painting. Chŏng Sŏn popularized the depiction of Korean scenery.

Kim Hong-do, better known by his sobriquet Tanwŏn, was perhaps the most prolific and versatile painter in the entire history of Korean painting. He worked as a court painter in the Painting Bureau and later was given an honorary title, *hyŏn'gam* (county magistrate). There is virtually no subject which he did not paint, but he was most famous for his genre paintings in which he recorded both faithfully and humorously the day-to-day life of the common people.

229. Ceremonial Procession

Attributed to Kim Hong-do (1745 - after 1814 A.D.)
Yi, Handscroll, ink and light colors on paper
H. 25.3 cm
National Museum of Korea

Reproduced here is a section of a long handscroll depicting a magnificent parade which took place in 1785 to welcome a new magistrate of Annŭng (present-day Naju or Anju). The entire parade included soldiers with banners, musical bands, military and civil officials, female servants, patrolmen, courtesans, palanquin carriers, and attendants of different ranks. The women shown in this section are identified as "female servants on horseback" by the two small characters above the head of the rider to the far right. All the women servants are wearing broad-rimmed traveling hats. Several take shelter under their *chang'ot*, a long cape-like outer garment worn by Korean women on their outings. Each female servant is accompanied by a groom.

The painting is composed of two horizontal registers in which the figures and horses are arranged in a frieze-like manner. Curiously, the figures and the animals in the upper register are much larger than those in the lower register. The artist may have added the lower register as an afterthought. Note that the head of the second woman from the left is awkwardly placed between the legs of the horse above her, to avoid any overlapping.

Although the painting is said to be by Kim Hong-do, the most famous figure and genre painter of the late Yi period, it lacks both the vitality and the specific detail which characterize Kim Hong-do's figure paintings. This could be a work by a lesser painter in the Painting Bureau who collaborated with Kim in a routine official production.

230 a-e. Women on Tano Day, Sword Dance, Party by the Lotus Pond, Boating Excursion and Collecting Alms on the Road
(For a and e see Colorplates XXXVII-XXXVIII)
By Sin Yun-bok (1758 A.D. - ?)
Yi, Five album leaves, ink and colors on paper
H. 28.2 cm (each)
Kansong Museum of Fine Arts

These are five leaves from an album of thirty in the collection of the Kansong Museum of Fine Arts. The Tano Day (fifth day of the fifth month, according to the lunar calendar) depicted in No. 230a is one of the most important Korean holidays. The celebration probably originated in ancient agricultural rites intended to insure a good harvest and drive away destructive insects and demons of plague. At this time people collect medicinal herbs, use demon-repelling charms and make offerings to the ancestors, powerful spirits able to affect the destiny of the living. Although the festival's occurrence on the fifth day of the fifth month and its association with ritual washing come from China, it is given a uniquely Korean flavor as a day of outdoor amusement, particularly for children and women. The latter emerge in colorful dress to swing on swings hung especially for the occasion. Here Sin Yun-bok depicts women swinging, arranging their hair and relaxing on a hillside while others, half-nude, bathe in a nearby stream. Although the bathers seem unaware of them, two monks, half-hidden behind a rock, are obviously delighted by the sight of naked women. This quality of light eroticism characterizes many of Sin's paintings, reminding us of the story he lost his position in the Painting Bureau due to his predilection for erotica.

In the *Sword Dance* two female dancers and a seven-man orchestra perform for an upper-class audience. The Korean sword dance was performed originally by men and is associated with an ancient legend about Hwang Ch'angnang, a professional wandering sword dancer in the kingdom of Silla. He became so famous that he was invited to perform before the king of Paekche, a neighboring and enemy kingdom. During that performance he killed the king with his sword. In retaliation Paekche had him executed, but his patriotism inspired the people of Silla to imitate the dance in his memory. Other points of interest in this painting are costume and hair styles, including the women's chignon hair pieces, and the smoking of tobacco, a custom introduced from Japan in the early 17th century. By using vivid purple, red and blue for the costumes Sin Yun-bok effectively makes them the focal point of the composition.

No. 230c depicts three gentlemen and their female companions enjoying the evening in a garden by a lotus pond. The woman on the right plays the *kayagŭm*, a twelve-stringed instrument invented in the 6th century by Urŭk, a famous musician of the Old Silla period. Sin Yun-bok's masterful handling of delicate brush lines and his use of subdued colors enhance the subtle mood of the evening. The artist inscribed the painting with a famous saying attributed to K'ung Jung (153 - 203 A.D.), a Chinese official put to death, with his entire family, by Ts'ao Ts'ao (155 - 220 A.D.):

My hall is always full of guests,
My wine cups are never empty.

In No. 230d three gentlemen and their female companions enjoy the music and cool summer breeze on the Han River, which flows along the southern edge of Seoul. Boating on the Han River was one of the favorite recreations of the upper classes in Sin Yun-bok's time. Behind the boat rises a rocky cliff which serves as the dramatic backdrop for the "stage" in front. As in the previous leaves, Sin Yun-bok has used a subdued color scheme appropriate for the scene. Against the predominantly blue background the light skin color of the figures appears particularly elegant. The artist's inscription reads:

I can't hear the flute in the evening breeze.

White gulls fly down before the waves.

No. 230e depicts an encounter on a mountainous road between a group of four men collecting alms and five women on an outing. Three women wear the *chang'ot*, a long cape-like outer garment worn mostly by Korean women. As one woman lifts her skirt and reaches for her *chumŏni* (purse) to donate money, a gentleman passing by looks back at her, a gesture with erotic overtones.

Sin Yun-bok was one of the most important Korean genre painters of the late Yi Dynasty. Both he and his father were court painters and both held the rank of *ch'ŏmsa* (a middle-ranking military official). The Yi practice of conferring honorary military titles on artists of the Painting Bureau was similar to that of the Ming court, where painters received honorary titles in the Embroidered Uniform Guard. In his genre painting Sin Yun-bok, unlike Kim Hong-do, preferred to depict courtesans and members of the upper classes enjoying their leisure time.

231. A Tiger
Anonymous, Yi (probably 18th century A.D.)
Hanging scroll, ink and light colors on silk
H. 96 cm
National Museum of Korea

The crouching pose of the tiger, tightly contained within the borders of the painting, emphasizes the power of the animal, also reflected in its large glaring eyes. Late Yi tiger paintings tend to be more naturalistic than contemporary Japanese tiger paintings. Korean artists may have based their work on actual observation, since tigers inhabited Korea in large numbers up until the early 20th century (a Korean subspecies still inhabits parts of Korea along the North Korea-China border as well as the modern Chinese province of Kirin and the Yenpien Korean Autonomous District). Worshipped for their physical strength and protective powers, from the earliest times they formed the center of a religious cult which still continues today. The tiger represents the mountain or earth spirit in popular belief and is associated with such *yin* aspects of nature and life as the night, the moon and fertility. As in China, the tiger came to assume guardianship over one of the directions, the West.

A similar tiger painting now in a private collection in Japan was the joint work of two Korean artists: Kim Hong-do (see Nos. 226-228), who painted the tiger, and Kang Se-hwang (see No. 232), who painted the pine tree. The animals in these two paintings are not identical. On close examination, Kim Hong-do's tiger appears more realistic, and the organic relationship between its head and body more convincing.

This painting was traditionally attributed to Sim Sa-jŏng (see No. 224) because the seal following the inscription reads Hyŏnjae, Sim's sobriquet. This attribution is no longer accepted, since the inscription's cyclical date corresponds either to 1714, when the artist was only eight years old, or to 1774, five years after his death.

232 a-c. Scenic Spots of Songdo
(For b and c see Colorplates XXXIX-XL)
By Kang Se-hwang (1713 - 1791 A.D.)
Yi, Three album leaves, ink and light colors on paper
H. 32.8 cm (each)
Dongwon Museum of Fine Arts

These three leaves belong to an album illustrating seventeen scenic spots in and around Songdo (Songdo, or Kaesŏng, fifty miles north of Seoul, was the capital of the Koryŏ Dynasty). They exhibit an interest in the spatial relationships of abstract forms and in the use of graded ink tones. Kang Se-hwang often experimented with bold arrangements of rocks. In some scenes they overlap in layers, creating a sense of spatial recession (see No. 232a). In others they appear leaning against one another or as isolated boulders, not integrated into the spatial structure of the mountains but instead appearing to float on top of them

(see No. 232b). Some elements in these compositions strike a Western viewer as surprisingly modern.
Each scene is identified by the artist. On No. 232a he writes:

White Stone Pool (Grotto) is along the way to Yŏngt'ong. White stones are like snow, square as the chess board. A clear stream flows down from above. Four mountains drip green color (because they're so intensely green). When I got there, a rain just stopped and it was clearing. The scenery was beyond compare. I cannot forget it every time (I recall it).

No. 232b depicts the entrance to Yŏngt'ong Grotto, which the artist describes in his inscription as follows:

At the entrance to Yŏngt'ong Grotto, stones are magnificent, large as houses. Green moss (creepers) covers them. My first impression was a shock. Someone said a dragon rose from the bottom of the pool, but I don't believe it (it does not appear so). But the great view ought to be rare.

No. 232c features "Clear Heart Lake."
Kang Se-hwang, born into a prominent scholar-official family, was well-versed in Chinese literature and skilled in the "three excellences" (samjŏl)—painting, calligraphy and poetry—the ideal accomplishments of the Confucian scholar. Familiar with Chinese literati painting theory and using literati styles in most of his own paintings, he was instrumental in the development of literati painting in Korea. He is also known for the comments he wrote on the paintings of his contemporaries and for his supervision of professional painters at court. In calligraphy he worked in the manner of the Chinese scholar-artists Wang Hsi-chih, Mi Fu and Chao Meng-fu. He carved seals in Han and T'ang styles. As a government official he was sent on a special mission to Peking in 1784. There his calligraphy and painting were greatly admired, and the Ch'ien-lung Emperor presented him with a tablet which read: Not as good as Mi [Fu] but better than Tung [Ch'i-ch'ang].

233. Mount Tobong
By Kim Sŏk-sin (1758 A.D. - ?)
Yi, Album leaf, ink and light colors on paper
H. 36.6 cm
Yi Dong-ju Collection

This leaf is from an album depicting the scenery around Mount Tobong and other mountains north of Seoul. Although the painting is loosely organized, the strong, dynamic brushwork lends it a surface unity and a sense of movement. The influence of the earlier academic painter Chŏng Sŏn (see Nos. 219-221) is obvious, especially in the use of jagged brushstrokes for the bony mountain peaks, sweeping horizontal strokes for the pine trees and scattered rocks along the stream. Nevertheless, the painting lacks the monumentality so often found in Chŏng Sŏn's works.
The practice of painting scenic spots in Korea was initiated, for the most part, by Chŏng Sŏn and was followed by such artists as Kim Ŭng-hwan, Kim Sŏk-sin and Ch'oe Puk, who were associated with the Painting Bureau. In such paintings the strong, sometimes even coarse, brushwork seems to be a sign of the artist's direct and spontaneous approach to nature.
Kim Sŏk-sin came from a family of professional painters which included Kim Ŭng-hwan (1742 - 1789 A.D.), teacher of the more celebrated painter Kim Hong-do (Nos. 226-229), and Sŏk-sin's brothers Tŭk-sin (No. 245) and Yang-sik.

234. A Plantain Tree and Rock
By King Chŏngjo (1752 - 1800 A.D.)
Yi
Hanging scroll, ink on paper
H. 84.6 cm
Dongkuk University Museum

King Chŏngjo (reigned 1776 - 1800 A.D.), the twenty-second king of the Yi Dynasty, received a typical royal education which included training in the practice of painting and calligraphy. This painting, a simple depiction of a plantain tree growing behind a garden rock, is an example of his work. Graded wet ink tones and touches of light blue describe the large leaves and garden rock. Variations in ink tone and nervous contour lines enliven the painting. One of the two seals reads Hongjae, the king's artist name.
During King Chŏngjo's reign Korea experienced a cultural renaissance. Confucian studies were revived, and many historical and literary materials were published, including the king's own collected works, containing some one hundred chapters. New ideas stimulated the scholarly community as a result of contact with the West through the Ch'ing China.

235. A Strolling Old Scholar
By Ch'oe Puk (active mid 18th century A.D.)
Yi, Album leaf, ink and light colors on paper
H. 30.6 cm
Lee Hurak Collection

An examination of Ch'oe Puk's work reveals that he painted in a wide range of styles, from a conventional literati manner to a more expressive and eccentric one. In this painting he uses jagged and spontaneous brushstrokes to depict an elderly gentleman strolling in a garden. The unusually thick application of ink describing the figure and trees suggests that the artist may have used a fingerpainting technique similar to the one used by the Chinese painter Kao Ch'i-p'ei (1672 - 1734 A.D.), one of the Yangchou eccentrics. The technique was not unknown at this time in Korea, for Sim Sa-jŏng (see No. 224) seems to have practiced it in some of his works.
Ch'oe Puk was known for his eccentric personality and love of wine. He was a professional painter who sold his paintings for a living, or exchanged them for wine. Although no Korean source refers to his affiliation with the Painting Bureau, a Japanese account mentions his position there as well as his use of the sobriquet Kŏgijae on a painting in Japan dated 1748. Another painting of his, an autumn landscape in the National Museum of Seoul, is dated 1757 and signed Samgijae. The dates on these two works indicate that Ch'oe was active during the middle of the 18th century.

236. Returning Home on a Windy and Snowy Night
By Ch'oe Puk (active mid 18th century A.D.)
Yi, Album: leaf, ink and light colors on paper
H. 55.1 cm
Lee Hurak Collection

In this album leaf Ch'oe Puk depicts in a quick, spontaneous manner a snowstorm at night, with trees bending in the wind and warmly clothed figures struggling to reach home. The chill of a storm in a snow-covered mountain valley is emphasized by vigorous brushstrokes, by the bare, wind-blown trees and by the harshness of the strongly contrasting shades of light and dark ink. A slight sense of warmth is interjected by the presence of a dog from a nearby cottage barking at the travelers, as though inviting them to his home.

237. Fishing on the River on a Spring Day
By Ch'oe Puk (active mid 18th century A.D.)
Yi, Album leaf, ink and light colors on paper
H. 66.3 cm
Lee Hurak Collection

Another example of Ch'oe's more expressive painting style, this leaf features a pavilion on a high plateau and an angler fishing in the river below. The artist combined rough brushwork and abbreviated forms with an interesting semi-circular composition in which the cliff across from the pavilion is flattened out and appears to be hanging precariously over it.

238. Mountains and Rivers Without End (Two Sections)
By Yi In-mun (1745 - 1821 A.D.)
Yi, Handscroll, ink and light colors on silk

H. 44.1 cm
National Museum of Korea

In this long handscroll where mountains and fishing villages are teeming with human activity, Yi In-mun combined several different styles: soft earthen hills with hemp-fiber texture strokes and small dots of the Chinese Tung-Chü tradition, as interpreted by early Ch'ing orthodox painters of China; rocks with large axe-cut texture strokes in the Chinese Ma-Hsia style; and rocky mountains in a sharp linear rendition recalling the style of Chinese Anhui masters such as Hung Jen (late 17th century).

The use of perspective, perhaps inspired by contact with European painting, is evident in the harbor section with its multitude of fishing boats which diminish in size and appear progressively blurred as they recede in space. Yi's use of mist is particularly successful in conveying the effect of atmospheric perspective. His handling of light colors, such as pale blue and light brown, is effective in conveying the freshness of the scenery.

The painting has several seals of Kim Chŏng-hŭi (see No. 240) and so presumably once belonged to his collection.

Yi In-mun was a court artist whose paintings display an unusually wide range of styles. He seems to have experimented with and absorbed many different elements from both the Northern and Southern School traditions in China. More direct inspiration, however, was supplied by works of Chŏng Sŏn (see Nos. 219-221), a pioneer in the depiction of local Korean scenery. Also noticeable in Yi In-mun's works is the influence of his contemporary Kim Hong-do (see Nos. 228-229), one of the most versatile Korean painters.

239. A Gathering of Four Friends
By Yi In-mun (1745 - 1821 A.D.).
Yi (dated 1820 A.D.)
Hanging scroll, ink and light colors on paper
H. 86.5 cm
National Museum of Korea

A pavilion is situated in a secluded mountainous setting. Behind the pavilion rises a series of steep rocky cliffs whose structure is not clearly defined. The somewhat disorderly arrangement of landscape elements is a common feature in other Korean landscapes of the post-Chŏng Sŏn era. Typically, small mountain peaks and rocks in these paintings appear to float by themselves, unencumbered by any force of gravity, creating a sense of dynamism amid confusion. In this painting the foreground trees and rocks seem more orderly and stable than those in the background.

This painting is one of Yi In-mun's late works, done, according to the inscription, when he was 76. The inscription also identifies the subject of the painting—a gathering of the artist and three friends in a pavilion surrounded by pine trees and a clear stream. The artist himself is shown unrolling a thick roll of paper, while a friend, the contemporary painter Im Hŭi-ji (identified by his sobriquet, Suwŏl), holds one end of the roll. The figure seated on the railing in one corner of the pavilion is Kim Yŏng-myŏn (the Chu-gyŏng of the inscription), a scholar-painter and famous ch'in player, whose instrument lies in front of him on the floor. The fourth figure, Yŏngsu, could be Im No (1755 - 1828 A.D.), a retired politician and scholar whose sobriquet was Yŏngsŏ kŏsa; he sits on a stool chanting a poem. Meanwhile, servants are preparing food outside the pavilion and in the corridor on the left.

The theme, a gathering of scholars, is a popular Chinese subject painted by generations of Chinese painters from the Northern Sung period on. Perhaps this is why Yi In-mun chose to depict the figures in Chinese dress.

240. Orchids
By Kim Chŏng-hŭi (1786 - 1857 A.D.)
Yi, Hanging scroll, ink on paper
H. 55 cm
Son Seki Collection

A typical example of Kim Chŏng-hŭi's painting, this hanging scroll is characterized by calligraphic overtones. The orchid petals were done using a combination of clerical (li-shu) and cursive (ts'ao-shu) styles, a fact Kim mentions in one of his inscriptions surrounding the plants. The orchids are described with long, flat strokes of ink, without any contour lines, their stems gently bending to the right. Some display the kind of fei-pai ("flying-white") broken brushstrokes used in calligraphy.

Stylistically, Kim Chŏng-hŭi's calligraphy underwent a series of changes during his lifetime due to the influence of different Chinese masters: Tung Ch'i-ch'ang (1555 - 1636 A.D.) of the late Ming; Weng Fang-kang (1733 - 1818 A.D.) of the Ch'ing; Su Shih (1037 - 1101 A.D.) and Mi Fu (1052 - 1107 A.D.) of the Northern Sung; and finally, Li Yung (678 - 747 A.D.) and Ou-yang Hsün (557 - 641 A.D.) of the T'ang Dynasty. His synthesis of these styles and his interest in the study of inscribed stone steles, then current in China, enabled him to develop a distinctive personal style known as the "Ch'usa ch'e" or the Ch'usa style (Ch'usa was his sobriquet). In some ways the style recalls that of Teng Shih-ju (1743 - 1805 A.D.) and I Ping-shou (1745 - 1815 A.D.) in its combination of the techniques of clerical script (li-shu) and seal script (chuan-shu). In Korea the Ch'usa style has always been described as kigoe, or novel and strange.

Kim Chŏng-hŭi was probably the most eminent scholar and calligrapher among the late Yi literati painters represented in this exhibition. Born in 1788, the eldest son of the prominent official Kim No-gyŏng (1766 - 1840 A.D.), Chŏng-hŭi was trained to carry on the family tradition in scholarship and government service. He passed the metropolitan civil service examination in 1819 and served in various government posts before he became Second Minister of Personnel in 1836.

Kim belonged to a group of scholars known as the Puk-hak p'a or Northern School, a branch of Sirhak (shih-hsüeh in Chinese) which advocated practical learning. It was through his contact with such prominent Ch'ing scholars as Weng Fang-kang (1733 - 1818 A.D.) and Juan Yüan (1764 - 1849 A.D.) that he further refined his study of calligraphy and epigraphy based on the Empirical Research School (K'ao-cheng hsüeh). He was well-versed in Chinese painting and calligraphy theory and left behind a substantial body of writings on the subject. Chŏng-hŭi also carved his own seals.

241. Plum Blossom Studio
By Cho Hŭi-ryong (1797 - 1859 A.D.)
Yi
Hanging scroll, ink and light colors on paper
H. 106.1 cm
Kansong Museum of Fine Arts

In this scroll a scholar, perhaps the artist himself, is admiring a plum branch in his studio. The studio in turn is surrounded by plum trees blossoming in the early spring snow. Bold brushwork, strong contrasts of dark ink against white background and the repeated application of white dots all contribute to create exciting visual effects.

The artist's inscription reads as follows:

In a waste basket I found a piece of old paper—a painting called "Viewing Plum Blossoms from a Study," done years ago. Although painted at will, it is full of wonder. Soot and smoke made the paper dark, almost a century old. A painting of plums like this . . . when I unroll it, I cannot help feeling that I have seen it in my previous existence.

The inscription ends with Cho's sobriquet, Tanno.

Cho Hŭi-ryong, a friend and close follower of the famous historian and calligrapher-painter Kim Chŏng-hŭi (see No. 240), was one of the leading scholar-painters of the early 19th century. He developed a personal mode of expression which departed from traditional painting styles.

Cho was particularly fond of painting plum blossoms, and his portrayals were admired for their lifelike quality. One anecdote which refers to this quality is about an immortal who dreamt that he lost one plum tree out of the ten thousand he grew in his garden. Cho was said to have stolen it and painted it into a plum blossom scroll. His fondness for plum blossoms extended to his adopting *Mae-su*, or Plum Blossom Old Man, as one of his sobriquets as well as to his naming his studio *Maehwa paegyŏngnu*, 100 Plum Blossoms Song Studio.

Among Cho Hŭi-ryong's writings, *Hosan Woesa* is an important source for the study of late Yi Dynasty painters.

242. Butterflies
By Cho Hŭi-ryong (1799 - 1859 A.D.)
Yi
Hanging scroll, ink and colors on paper
H. 129 cm
National Museum of Korea

Cho Hŭi-ryong also excelled in orchid and butterfly paintings. In this scroll flowers and different types of butterflies, in varying sizes and colors, are carefully arranged on the picture surface, which is decorated with small patches of gold and silver paper. Cho Hŭi-ryong was among a limited number of Yi Dynasty artists who painted this subject. Another well-known butterfly painter was Nam Kye-u (1811 - 1888 A.D.), often called Nam Nabi or Butterfly Nam. In contrast to Cho's butterflies, those in Nam's paintings usually are depicted with flowers in natural settings.

A long inscription by Cho reveals the influence of his friend Kim Chŏng-hŭi's calligraphic style. It reads:

The Prince of T'eng, [Li] Yüan-ying, specialized in painting butterflies. His name has been handed down for a thousand autumns. The butterflies in his paintings cannot be seen. Those in the courtyard can be seen every day. So the butterflies in this painting resemble those in the courtyard. Why would one want (images of) butterflies in one's painting(s)? To let it be known that their loftiness and beauty extends to this. Now I will record on my butterfly painting a strange tale about a Hsün butterfly. In the Court of Imperial Sacrifices in Peking there was a butterfly, yellow in color and large as a tea bowl in size. Wishing to see it, an official called it by its name, "Lao-tao," and it flew onto his palm. When he was about to harm it, the butterfly flew away. This story has been handed down for more than two hundred years, from the Chia-ching era (1522 - 1567 A.D.) of the Ming Dynasty to the present. And thus the butterfly also has had a long life.
On a summer day in the Tamhwa Cottage, I jot down these random comments.

The Prince of T'eng, Li Yüan-ying, was the twenty-second son of the founder of the T'ang Dynasty (618 - 906 A.D.). His palace in Kiangsi is the subject of a famous poem by Wang P'o (650 - 676 A.D.), "The Pavilion of the Prince of T'eng." The prince is mentioned in this inscription because he was one of the first recorded butterfly painters in China.

243. Leisurely Conversation Under Pine Trees
By Kim Su-ch'ŏl (active mid 19th century A.D.)
Yi, Album leaf, ink and light colors on paper
H. 33.1 cm
Kansong Museum of Fine Arts

Five scholars are engaged in leisurely conversation beneath a group of pine trees. Figures, trees and rocks are defined by sketchy contour lines, light dots and short brushstrokes. Soft washes in a warm-cool color palette enhance tree trunks, foliage and rocks along the stream, imbuing the painting with a gentle poetic mood. Kim's painting style may be compared with the Nanga style of 18th and 19th century Japan. Two of the artist's seals appear on this leaf.

Among the individualist painters active in the 19th century, Kim Su-ch'ŏl was noted for his very personal interpretations of nature in terms of simple forms and delicate colors. Accomplished in both landscape and flower painting, Kim's landscapes reveal the stylistic influence of the scholar-painter Yun Che-hong (1764 - 1840 A.D.).

Although the painter's exact dates are unknown, two of his extant paintings bear the dates 1849 and 1850. Some of

his works bear inscriptions by scholar-painters such as Cho Hŭi-ryong (see Nos. 241-242) and Kim Chŏng-hŭi (see No. 240). Two of the artist's seals appear on this leaf.

244 a-b. Flowers
By Kim Su-ch'ŏl (active mid 19th century A.D.)
Yi, Pair of hanging scrolls, ink and colors on paper
H. 127.9 cm (each)
National Museum of Korea

Here flowers are growing from the edges of garden rocks. While Kim uses some outlines to depict the rocks, his brushwork is predominantly in the *mo-ku* or "boneless" manner, characterized by washes of varying tones of ink and light color. The artist's interest in the overall harmony of color and form is again apparent here in the light brushstrokes and combination of warm and cool colors, without any emphasis on the realistic appearance of flowers or rocks. The decorative quality of the painting is enhanced by the paper, which is covered with patches of gold leaf.

245. Blacksmiths
By Kim Tŭk-sin (1754 - 1822 A.D.)
Yi, Album leaf, ink and light colors on paper
H. 22.5 cm
Kansong Museum of Fine Arts

In this painting three blacksmiths are working on a piece of hot iron in a spacious, open area in front of a thatched shed. A fourth figure, a young apprentice, looks nonchalantly over the shoulder of the squatting figure who looks at the viewer instead of giving his full attention to the piece of hot iron he holds in place for his co-workers, who take turns pounding it down. Thus the hard work of the blacksmith appears pleasant and unhurried.

Kim Tŭk-sin used a minimal number of lines to indicate drapery folds, adopting a simplicity of style appropriate to his theme. His masterful handling of the brush is particularly noticeable in the delineation of the bare torso of the youthful worker on the right.

Genre scenes such as this were painted exclusively by professional painters at court and not by scholar-painters of the period.

Kim Tŭk-sin was a court painter who specialized in figure and genre scenes. His achievements in genre painting have been overshadowed by those of his more famous contemporaries, Kim Hong-do (see Nos. 226-229) and Sin Yun-bok (see No. 230), both of whose extant works outnumber those of Kim Tŭk-sin. Kim Tŭk-sin's paintings, however, are often characterized by greater intimacy and humor.

246. Women
By Yu Un-hong (1797 - 1859 A.D.)
Yi, Album leaf, ink and light colors on paper
H. 23.9 cm
Lee Hurak Collection

Three women appear on a *t'oemmaru* (a narrow wooden porch) frequently seen in the courtyards of Korean-style houses. The doors of the rooms behind and to the left, with their elaborate lattice work, provide a shallow intimate spatial setting. One of the women smokes a long bamboo pipe with a small metal tip. Courtesans smoking pipes also appear in Sin Yun-bok's paintings (see No. 230). By the 18th century pipe smoking seems to have become popular even among female entertainers. Also noteworthy is the extremely short length of the *chŏgori* (Korean blouse). The length of the *chŏgori* is one of the major variables in Korean fashion. The women's faces are devoid of any specific expressions, and their drapery lines are harsh and mannered.

The artist's signature, Sisan (his sobriquet), appears in the lower left corner.

Scenes depicting courtesans and women in household settings were popularized first by Sin Yun-bok (see No. 230), who greatly influenced Yu Un-hong.

Little is known about Yu Un-hong, a court painter of the

late Yi period. He held the military rank *ch'ŏmsa,* often given to court painters as an honorary title.

247. Portrait of Kang Yi-o (1788 A.D. - ?)
By Yi Chae-gwan (1783 - 1837 A.D.)
Yi, Hanging scroll, ink and colors on silk
H. 63.9 cm
National Museum of Korea

Kang Yi-o is portrayed here in a formal frontal pose wearing his official robe *(kwanbok),* and winged, silk *samo* hat. The meticulous description of the shaded patterns of the hat and the characterization of the face reveal the artist's efforts to describe both the personality and the official position of Kang Yi-o.

Unlike most official portraits, this one was signed by the artist, Yi Chae-gwan (or So-dang), who entitled it "True Likeness of Yaksan" (Yaksan was Kang Yi-o's sobriquet). In the upper right corner is an inscription by Kim Chŏng-hŭi (see No. 240) which reads:

> *His appearance is so cleverly done that the portrait looks just like the real official. This is because it (the painting) is so strikingly lifelike. Who better knew the curves and lines of heaven and earth and netted them within heart and breast? Whatever [Kang Yi-o] encountered, [he did so] with spirit.*
> *Inscribed by Noyŏm (Kim Chŏng-hŭi)*

Kang Yi-o, the grandson of the artist Kang Se-hwang (see No. 232), was an accomplished painter. He passed the government examinations and became a local magistrate.

248. Traveling Along the Riverside
By Paek Ŭn-bae (1820 - after 1894 A.D.)
Yi, Album leaf, ink and colors on paper
H. 26.4 cm
Kansong Museum of Fine Arts

A scholar on a donkey is traveling through a mountain canyon, accompanied by his boy servant. The artist has captured the figures at the moment when they stop to look at a pair of wild ducks. Even the donkey seems to be watching these birds. The scholar's costume is typically Korean and includes the *kat,* a traditional high hat made of horse hair and tied under the chin with two strings. The rocky cliffs and path create a tightly interlocking composition. Their sharp lines contrast with the softer, more undulating lines of the figures and animal. The artist's sobriquet, Yimdang, appears on the right along with two of his seals.

Paek Ŭn-bae served as a court painter for more than 40 years. At the age of 75 he supposedly painted a screen of one hundred folding panels which still displayed vigorous brushwork and fine details, despite his advanced age. Although the majority of his extant works are figure paintings, he was also famous for his landscape and animal paintings. He is one of the major painters of the 19th century who continued the Kim Hong-do genre tradition (see Nos. 226-229).

249. Swimming Ducks
By Hong Se-sŏp (1831 A.D. - ?)
Yi, Hanging scroll, ink on paper
H. 119.5 cm
National Museum of Korea

In this hanging scroll the bird's-eye view of the pair of swimming ducks is a daring compositional device, reminiscent of Kim Sik's use of perspective in No. 195. The painter ingeniously used varied grades of dark and light strips of ink to depict rippling water, creating a sense of movement.

Born into a family of scholars, Hong Se-sŏp belonged to a group of innovative painters active in the latter part of the 19th century. A specialist in bird-and-flower painting, he probably learned to paint from his father, with whom he collaborated on joint projects. Their styles were so similar that their works often could not be told apart.

250. A Gentleman Watching Geese

By Chang Sŭng-ŏp (1843 - 1897 A.D.)
Yi, Hanging scroll, ink and light colors on silk
H. 143.5 cm
Kim Hyong-tae Collection

A scholar and his servant are perched on boulders watching geese in a marshy pool below. This foreground scene is separated from a pavilion and rocky promontory on the left and mountains peaks in the distance by a diagonal band of mist. Rocks are described by outlining, shading and overlapping, the latter especially pronounced in the sharply faceted rocks beneath the pavilion. Figures are defined with tremulous outlines and delicate features; particularly noticeable are the scholar's long, thin hands and rather aloof expression. All these features are reminiscent of the landscape and figure styles of the Chinese painter Ts'ui Tzu-chung (d. 1644 A.D.), active during the late Ming period in Peking, where Koreans may have encountered his work.

The gentleman watching geese in this painting is identified in the inscription as the Chinese scholar and calligrapher Wang Hsi-chih (321 - 379 A.D.). Famous for his cursive script *(ts'ao-shu),* he admired geese for the gracefulness of their long necks, a quality he felt could be captured in calligraphy. The inscription refers to the rare geese he acquired once in exchange for a copy he agreed to make of a Taoist text. The artist did not write the inscription himself (most of the inscriptions on Chang Sŭng-ŏp's paintings were written by better-educated friends).

251. Homecoming
By Chang Sŭng-ŏp (1843 - 1897 A.D.)
Yi (dated 1890 A.D.)
Hanging scroll, ink and light colors on paper
H. 136.5 cm
Kansong Museum of Fine Arts

Now mounted as a hanging scroll, this painting was originally one of ten panels of a folding screen. In the foreground a boat approaches the shore, where a servant is waiting for the scholar to disembark. Farther back an open gate leads to a cottage, secluded in this rustic setting. Finally mountains rise in the background, closing off the painting in the upper part of the scroll. Despite the upward movement of trees and mountains, the major emphasis is on the horizontal disposition of elements, lending the scroll a static quality.

The inscribed title, "Homecoming," identifies the theme as the famous poem by T'ao Yüan-ming (365 - 427 A.D.) describing his return home after retiring, disillusioned, from government service. Although some artists used this poem to allude to their own lives, it became one of the stock literary themes illustrated in painting.

This painting, dated 1890, was done late in the artist's life. Its style, however, places it in a category with his earlier, more conservative works, usually in the manner of the literati painters of Yüan and Ming China. Another painting from the set of ten bears an inscription saying it is in the style of Wang Meng of the Yüan Dynasty (1279 - 1368 A.D.). Chang worked in both the orthodox literati tradition, as here, and in a more expressive, individualistic manner (No. 252).

Chang Sŭng-ŏp, whose sobriquet was Owŏn, was one of the last significant painters of the Yi Dynasty. Orphaned when young, he was forced to wander in his youth looking for work, often finding it in the homes of government officials. He became known for his artistic talent and his brilliant memory, which allowed him to copy paintings he had seen only once. His fame soon reached the court, and the king invited him to work there as a court painter.

252. Eagles
By Chang Sŭng-ŏp (1843 - 1897 A.D.)
Yi, Hanging scroll, ink and light colors on paper
H. 135.5 cm
Hoam Art Museum

This hanging scroll is one of a pair in the Hoam Art

Museum; the second scroll is of pheasants. Here two eagles, one poised to strike, are perched on branches which extend from one side of the scroll to the other, the tree trunk itself rising vertically along the left edge. The vigorous, fluid brushwork and accents of dark ink emphasize the strength and agility of these birds of prey. The artist's seal appears at the end of a two-line inscription in cursive script describing the lofty spirit of the eagles as they look down upon the vast autumn fields and towering mountains below:

> The vast earth and high mountains increase my will to fly.
> Withered maples and falling leaves heighten my spirit.

Chang Sŭng-ŏp drew upon a long tradition of Korean eagle painting done in a manner related to the "boneless" (mo-ku) style, using washes of ink and no outline. Earlier examples include works by Cho Sok (1598 - 1668) and Sim Sa-jŏng, a scholar-painter of the 18th century (see No. 224). The ultimate sources of these Korean eagle paintings were undoubtedly the ink monochrome paintings by the Chinese Che School painter Lin Liang (active 1488 - 1515 A.D.) of the early Ming period.

253. Visiting the Peach Blossom Spring
By An Chung-sik (1861 - 1919 A.D.)
Modern (dated 1913 A.D.)
Hanging scroll, ink and colors on silk
H. 164.4 cm
Hoam Art Museum

This hanging scroll, dated 1913, illustrates a famous composition by the 5th century Chinese scholar-official and poet T'ao Yüan-ming, the "Peach Blossom Spring" (for illustration of a poem by T'ao Yüan-ming see No. 251). This work tells of a fisherman who was winding his way along a stream bordered by blossoming peach trees when he happened upon an ideal community. The community had been founded several hundred years earlier by people fleeing the tyranny of the Ch'in Dynasty (221 - 207 B.C.) and had remained isolated from the rest of the world ever since.

An Chung-sik depicts the lone fisherman as he follows the grove of peach trees in his boat before discovering the Peach Blossom Spring settlement, visible in the left middle ground at the end of a winding stream, surrounded by huge boulders. The landscape elements consist of jagged, monumental mountain forms depicted in blue and green mineral pigments, a Chinese landscape painting style which goes back at least to the T'ang Dynasty (618 - 906 A.D.).

An Chung-sik, a student of Chang Sŭng-ŏp (see Nos. 249-252), was one of the most important painters active at the turn of the century. His painting belongs to the last stage of the long Yi Dynasty painting tradition. At the age of twenty he went to China with one hundred technicians sent there to learn how to make and use new weapons. He also traveled to Japan to widen his artistic views. Though not a court painter, he painted portraits of the late Yi kings. In his late years he taught painting at the Sŏhwa Misurwŏn, or Academy of Calligraphy and Painting, the training ground for official painters during the Japanese occupation of Korea.

254. Elegant Gathering at Mount Tobong
By Yi Yong-wu (1902 - 1952 A.D.)
Modern, Album leaf, ink and colors on paper
H. 33 cm
Lee Hurak Collection

A group of gentlemen is gathered to view antiquities at a scenic spot in the mountains. Three of the men are admiring scrolls while four others are seated around ceramic objects. Removed from these two groups are two servants preparing tea. Such outings were common among the Korean literati and were occasions for socializing with friends, enjoying the natural scenery, viewing art and writing or painting in commemoration of the event. The artist does not identify the scholars as particular individuals with any distinguishing features, although he does portray them in Korean dress.

The mountain peaks are defined by swift horizontal

strokes, their leftward thrust balanced by the rapid movement of the stream toward the right. Because of his interest in experimenting with unusual forms and colors in landscape painting, Yi was considered eccentric by his contemporaries.

Yi Yong-wu was another painter whose work is representative of one aspect of mid 20th century artistic trends in Korea. He specialized in landscape and bird-and-flower painting, the latter in a style influenced by the modern Chinese painter Wu Ch'ang-shih (1842 - 1937 A.D.).

255. Landscape
By Yi Sang-bŏm (1897 - 1972 A.D.)
Modern, Panel, ink and light colors on paper
H. 77 cm
Hoam Art Museum

This painting belongs to a late, mature period in Yi Sang-bŏm's artistic career, when he frequently depicted long horizontal landscapes with stretches of shallow streams and low-lying mountains and hills which gradually become obscured by mist. Landscape forms are constructed of short texture strokes related to the axe-cut variety. Yi's paintings convey the spirit of nature and the artist's humble attitude toward it.

Yi Sang-bŏm was a modern Korean painter active until 1972. His painting education began when he was seventeen and studied under An Chung-sik (see No. 253) at the Sŏhwa Misurwŏn, the Academy of Calligraphy and Painting. As a professional painter he worked on government projects, such as murals for the Ch'angdŏk Palace, and at other times in his career he worked as an art reporter and painting teacher.

His paintings reveal the influence of his teacher An Chung-sik (he even borrowed the second character of An's sobriquet, Simjŏn, for that of his own, Ch'ŏngjŏn). Some Japanese elements are detectable in the works of his middle period, during the Japanese occupation of Korea. Of the painters of modern Korea who carried on traditional painting styles, Yi Sang-bŏm was one of the most successful.

256. Autumn Colors on Samsŏn Peak in the Diamond Mountains
By Pyŏn Kwan-sik (1899 - 1976 A.D.)
Modern (dated 1959 A.D.)
Panel, ink and light colors on paper
H. 156 cm
Kim Jong-ha Collection

Samsŏn-am or "Crag of the Three Immortals" is a famous spot in the Diamond Mountains, a range stretching from the north central part of Korea to the east coast. The range has long been a popular pilgrimage site and painting subject because of the thousands of needle-pointed, crystalline peaks and the spectacular views; the seasonal variety of flora and fauna; and the great number of temples. Here the sharp peaks extend into the distance while the three Immortals' Crag juts up from just left of center to dominate the scene. The artist, Pyŏn Kwan-sik, was known for his non-conformist, rigid personality, often reflected in his powerful brushwork, made up of short, dry texture strokes. He tended to paint typical Korean rural scenery and famous spots, such as the Samsŏn-am.

A contemporary of Yi Sang-bŏm, Pyŏn Kwan-sik, like Yi, was a modern painter working in traditional styles whose career spanned much of the first three quarters of this century. He entered the Academy of Calligraphy and Painting (Sŏhwa Misurwŏn) in 1916 and studied there for seven years under his maternal grandfather, Cho Sŏk-chin (1853 - 1920 A.D.). Cho, one of the last court painters of the Yi Dynasty, was a contemporary of An Chung-sik (1861 - 1919 A.D.). Both were active during the transitional period from late Yi to early Modern. Pyŏn continued his art education in Japan when he went to study at the Ueno Art School with Gomaro Suiun in 1925. He returned to Korea in 1929.

FURTHER READING

History and Archaeology

Chapin, Helen
"Kyŏngju; ancient capital of Silla." *Asian Horizon* 1 no.4:36-45. Winter 1948.

Chard, Chester S.
Northeast Asia in prehistory. Madison, The University of Wisconsin Press, 1974.

Gardiner, Kenneth Herbert James
The early history of Korea; the historical development of the peninsula up to the introduction of Buddhism in the fourth century A.D. Honolulu, University of Hawaii Press, 1969.

Han, Pyŏng-sam
"Neolithic culture of Korea." *Korea Journal* 14 no.4:12-17. April 1974.

Han, Woo-Keun
The history of Korea. Seoul, Eul-Yoo Pub. Co., 1970.

Hatada, Takashi
A history of Korea. Santa Barbara, American Bibliographical Center, 1969.

Kim, Jeong-hak
The prehistory of Korea. Honolulu, University Press of Hawaii, 1978.

Kim, Jung-bae
"Bronze age culture in Korea." *Korea Journal* 14 no.4:18-31. April 1974.

Kim, Wŏn-yong
"Dolmens in Korea." *Korean Research Center, Seoul. Bulletin; journal of social sciences and humanities* 16:1-11. June 1962.

—.
"Korea: new lights on Korean archaeology." *Asian Perspectives* 10:39-55. 1967.

Kim, Wŏn-yong and Richard Pearson
"Three royal tombs: new discoveries in Korean archaeology." *Archaeology* 30 no.5:302-314. Sept. 1977.

Korea (Republic). Ministry of Culture and Information.
A handbook of Korea. Seoul, Korean Overseas Information Service, Ministry of Culture and Information, 1978.

Pearson, Richard
"Japan, Korea, and China: the problem of defining continuities." *Asian Perspectives* 19 no.1:176-189.

—.
"Prehistoric subsistence and economy in Korea: an initial sketch." *Asian Perspectives* 17 no. 2:93-101. 1975.

—., ed.
The traditional culture and society of Korea: prehistory. Honolulu, Center for Korean Studies, University of Hawaii, 1975. (Occasional papers of the Center for Korean Studies, University of Hawaii, no. 3)

Reischauer, Edwin Oldfather and John Fairbank
East Asia, the great tradition. Boston, Houghton Mifflin, 1960. (A history of East Asian civilization, vol. 1)

Sohn, Pow-key, Kim Chol-choon and Hong Yi-sup
The history of Korea. Seoul, Korean National Commission for Unesco, 1970.

Taehan, Min-guk
"Republic of Korea." IN *Worldmark encyclopedia of the nations: Asia and Australia.* 4th ed. New York, Worldmark Press, John Wiley, 1971. p. 189-196.

Art and Culture

Forman, Werner
The art of ancient Korea. Text by Barinka. London, Peter Nevill, 1962.

Gompertz, Godfrey St. George Montague
"Korea" and "Korean art." IN *Encyclopedia of world art.* New York [etc.] McGraw-Hill, 1963. Vol. VIII, p. 1019-1028.

Ha, Tae-hung
Guide to Korean culture. Seoul, Yonsei University Press [distributed by Paragon Book Gallery, New York] 1968.

Kadokawa Shoten, eds.
A pictorial encyclopedia of the Oriental arts, Korea. New York, Crown, 1969.

Kim, Chewon
"Korea." IN *The art of Burma, Korea, Tibet,* by Alexander B. Griswold [et al.] New York, Crown, 1964. p. 61-149.

—.
"Treasures from the Songyim-sa temple in southern Korea." *Artibus Asiae* 22 nos. 1/2:95-112. 1959.

Kim, Chewon and Kim Wŏn-yong
Treasures of Korean art; 2000 years of ceramics, sculpture, and jeweled arts. New York, Abrams, 1966.

Kim, Chewon and Lena Kim Lee
Arts of Korea. Tokyo, Kodansha Interational, 1974.

Kim, Wŏn-yong
"Some aspects of the interrelation of Korean, Chinese and Japanese arts." *Korea Journal* 17 no.11:10-14. November 1977.

"Korea."
IN *The image of the Buddha,* ed. by David L. Snellgrove. Paris, Kodansha International [and] Unesco, 1978. p. 226-238.

Korea; its land, people and culture of all ages.
Seoul, Hakwon-sa Ltd., 1960.

Korea (Republic). Ministry of Culture and Information.
The arts of ancient Korea. Seoul, Kwang Myong Pub. Co., 1974.

Korea (Republic). Ministry of Education.
Masterpieces of Korean art; an exhibition . . . ed. by Robert T. Paine, Jr. Washington, 1957.

McCune, Evelyn
The arts of Korea; an illustrated history. Rutland, Vt., C. E. Tuttle, 1962.

Seckel, Dietrich
The art of Buddhism. New York, Crown, 1964. (Art of the world)

—.
"Some characteristics of Korean art." *Oriental Art* ns 23 no.1:52-61. Spring 1977.

Seoul. National Museum of Korea.
5000 years of Korean arts. Seoul, National Museum of Korea, 1976. Text in Korean and English.

—.
Guide book . . . 2nd rev. ed. Seoul, 1968.

Swann, Peter Charles
Art of China, Korea, and Japan. New York, Praeger, 1963. (Praeger world of art series)

Yanagi, Soetsu
"The mystery of beauty; a tribute to the Korean craftsman." *Far Eastern Ceramic Bulletin* 9 nos.3/4:6-11. (Serial no. 38) Sept. - Dec. 1957.

Buddhism

Finegan, Jack
The archaeology of world religions. Princeton, Princeton University Press, 1952.

Lee, Peter H.
Lives of eminent Korean monks: the Haedong Kosŭng Chŏn. Cambridge, Mass., Harvard University Press, 1969. (Harvard Yenching Institute   tudies 25)

Paik, Nak-choon
"Tripitaka Koreana." *Transactions of the Korean Branch of the Royal Asiatic Society* 32:62-73. 1951.

Starr, Frederick
Korean Buddhism; history–condition–art . . . Boston, Marshall Jones Co., 1918.

Trollope, Bishop Mark Napier
"Introduction to the study of Buddhism in Korea." *Transactions of the Korea Branch of the Royal Asiatic Society* 8:1-41. 1917.

Zürcher, Erik
Buddhism; its origin and spread in words, maps and pictures. London, Routledge & Kegan Paul, 1962.

Painting

Ahn Hwi-Joon
"Two Korean landscape paintings of the first half of the sixteenth century." *Korea Journal* 15 no.2:31-41. Feb. 1975.

Cox, Susan
"Unusual album by a Korean painter Kang Se-Whang." *Oriental Art* ns 19 no.2:156-168. Summer 1973.

Davidson, Joseph Leroy
"An unpublished Korean album." *Bulletin of the New York Public Library* 39:595-604. 1935.

Gazzard, Barry
"Korean Buddhist painting." *Oriental Art* ns 15 no.4:263-268. Winter 1969.

Lee, Lena Kim
"Chŏng Sŏn: a Korean landscape-painter." *Apollo* ns 88:84-93. Aug. 1968.

Loehr, Max
"An eleventh-century Korean copy of the Pi-Tsang-Ch'üan." IN HIS *Chinese landscape woodcuts.* Cambridge, Harvard University Press, 1968. Chapter IV, p. 55-69.

Pak, Young-sook
"Ksitigarbha as supreme lord of the underworld; a Korean Buddhist painting in the Museum für Ostasiatische Kunst in Berlin." *Oriental Art* ns 23 no.1:96-104. Spring 1977.

Umehara, Sueji
"The newly discovered tombs with wall paintings of Kao-kou-li dynasty." *Archives of the Chinese Art Society of America* 6:5-17. 1952.

Sculpture

Hwang, Su-yŏng
"Gilt-bronze images of Buddha in Korea with stress on personal collections." *Korea Journal* 10 no.7:7-10. July 1970.

Kim, Wŏn-yong
"An early gilt-bronze seated Buddha from Seoul." *Artibus Asiae* 23 no.1:67-71. 1960.

Lefebvre d'Argencé, René-Yvon, ed.
Chinese, Korean and Japanese Sculpture in The Avery Brundage Collection. San Francisco, Asian Art Museum of San Francisco, 1974.

Soper, Alexander Coburn
Chinese, Korean and Japanese bronzes . . . Rome, Istituto Italiano per il Medio ed Estremo Oriente, 1966. (Serie Orientale Roma, 35)

Tomita, Kojiro
"A Korean statue of the healing Buddha, eighth century." *Bulletin of the Museum of Fine Arts, Boston* 31:37-38. (Serial no. 185) June 1933.

Watson, William
"The earliest Buddhist images of Korea." *Transactions of the Oriental Ceramic Society* (London) 31:83-92. 1957-59.

Ceramics and Applied Arts

Akaboshi, Goro and Heiichiro Nakamaru
Five centuries of Korean ceramics, pottery and porcelain of the Yi dynasty. New York, Weatherhill/Tankosha, 1975.

Choi, Sunu
Korean ceramics in the National Museum of Korea. Tokyo, Kodansha, 1976. (*Tōyō tōji taikan,* vol. 2)

Figgess, John
"Mother of pearl inlaid lacquer of the Koryŏ dynasty." *Oriental Art* ns 23 no.1:87-95. Spring 1977.

Fontein, Jan
"Masterpieces of lacquer and metalwork." *Apollo* ns 88:114-119. Aug. 1968.

Gompertz, Godfrey St. George Montague
"The appeal of Korean celadon." *Oriental Art* ns 23 no.1:62-67. Spring 1977.

—.
Korean celadon and other wares of the Koryŏ period. New York, Thomas Yoseloff, 1964.

—.
Korean pottery and porcelain of the Yi period. New York, Praeger, 1968.

—.
"Seventeen centuries of Korean pottery." *Apollo* ns 88:104-113. Aug. 1968.

—.
"A trip through southern Korea (paper read . . . on 17th March 1965)." *Transactions of The Oriental Ceramic Society* 36:1-20. 1964/66.

Gray, Basil
"The inlaid metalwork of Korea." *British Museum Quarterly* 20:92-95. 1956.

Griffing, Robert P., Jr.
The art of the Korean potter . . . catalogue of an exhibition selected by Robert P. Griffing, Jr. and shown in Asia House Gallery in the spring of 1968. New York, The Asia Society, dist. by New York Graphic Society, 1968.

—.
"Some Koryŏ celadons in the collection of the Honolulu Academy of Arts." *Oriental Art* ns 23 no.1:68-79. Spring 1977.

Henderson, Gregory
"Dated late Koryŏ celadons: new finds and new theory." *Far Eastern Ceramic Bulletin* 9 no.2:1-7. Dec. 1959.

—.
Korean ceramics; an art's variety . . . Feb. 9 to March 9, 1969, Divisions of Art Gallery, The Ohio State University. Columbus, 1969.

Honey, William Bowyer
The ceramic art of China and other countries of the Far East. London, Faber & Faber, 1945.

—.
Korean pottery. London, Faber and Faber, 1947.

Kim Chewon and Godfrey St. G. M. Gompertz
The ceramic art of Korea. London, Faber & Faber, 1961.

Korean ceramics. Constitutes the entire issue of *Far Eastern Ceramic Bulletin* 9 nos.3-4 (Serial no. 38) Sept. - Dec. 1957.

Koyama, Fujio and John Figgess
Two thousand years of Oriental ceramics. London, Thames and Hudson, 1961.

Lee, Yu-kuan (Sammy)
"Korean lacquerware." IN HIS *Oriental lacquer art.* New York, Weatherhill, 1972.

Medley, Margaret
"Korea, China and Liao in Koryŏ ceramics." *Oriental Art* ns 23 no.1:80-86. Spring 1977.

—.
Korean and Chinese ceramics from the 10th to the 14th century . . . a loan exhibition mounted jointly by The Fitzwilliam Museum, Cambridge and The Percival David Foundation of Chinese Art . . . in The Fitzwilliam Museum . . . Cambridge, 1975.

Reynolds, Valrae
"Korean pottery in the Newark Museum." *Arts of Asia* 2 no.5:29-37. Sept.-Oct. 1972.

Syracuse University. Joe and Emily Lowe Art Center.
The John R. Fox collection of Korean ceramics, by Charles Ryder Dibble. Syracuse, 1965.

Tomita, Kojiro
"Korean silver-work of the Koryŏ period, a plaque." *Bulletin of the Museum of Fine Arts, Boston* 39:1-6. (Serial no. 231) Feb. 1941.

Miscellaneous

Kim, Chewon
"The stone pagoda of Koo Huang-li in South Korea." *Artibus Asiae* 13 nos.1/2:25-38. 1950.

Lee, Kyu
"Aspects of Korean architecture." *Apollo* ns 88:94-103. Aug. 1968.

Lee, Sang-beck
Hangŭl: the origin of the Korean alphabet according to new historical evidence. Seoul, Tong-Mun Kwan, 1957. (Publication of the National Museum of Korea, series A, vol. III)
Text in Korean with English summary.

MacGovern, Melvin Peter
Specimen pages of Korean movable types. Los Angeles, Dawson's Book Shop, 1966.

Sohn, Pow-key
"Early Korean printing." *Journal of the American Oriental Society* 79 no.2:96-103. April - June 1959.

Yi, Du-hyŏn
"Mask-dance drama." IN *Survey of Korean arts: folk arts.* Seoul, National Academy of Arts, 1974. p. 137-165.